Alters

Book One
of the "Lola, Party of Eight" series

by ERIN LEE

Dedications

For the alters who live inside each of us. May we celebrate your differences and encourage your spunk, creativity, and intelligence.

Also for our hosts, who never quit despite the mixed messages.

Lastly, for Nire.

Author's Note

I knew I was being a little overambitious when I set out to write a book about a woman with dissociative identity disorder (DID). It's challenging enough to write about one person's lives, thoughts, hopes, and dreams. Try doing it for eight people, all in the same body. However, after months of talking to people who suffer from DID, I felt it was a challenge worth taking on. Formerly known as multiple personality disorder and brought into pop culture after the famous Sybil case, DID is a psychological condition where portions of a person's personality split or splinter to help cope with trauma. These splits take on lives and personalities of their own, causing for interesting but confusing lives for the person with the condition.

Even with a background in psychology, I've had trouble understanding what it would be like to live with multiple personalities. And, in talking to those with DID, I realize their struggles are very real; multiplied by all the personalities living in them who struggle too. The challenges they face are bigger than I first suspected. Many people with DID told me they don't trust therapists because we *do* have such a hard time accepting their experiences. For this reason, I wanted even more to understand. I make no claim that I fully understand this disorder. However, I emphasize with those who have DID and hope Lola's story will help in spreading awareness and hope.

In order to appreciate this condition, it's important to first know the terminology associated with DID and other, often co-occurring, pathologies. I'm including a cheat sheet to these terms to help readers make sense of some of the terms they may not be familiar with.

Likewise, I'm adding a list of my main character—Lola's—alter egos so that readers can refer back in the event of confusion; which is bound to occur as result of the conversations, stories, and thoughts of eight people in one body. Please refer to them as often as needed, as it's something Lola herself would do. It's not easy keeping track of so many personalities!

DID is a chronic psychological illness. A person with DID plays host to two or more personalities called alters. Each alter has its own personality and may even have its own name. These alter egos often take turns controlling a person's behavior; several people sharing the same body.

DID occurs about eight times more frequently in women than in men and many believe that because DID can cause people to be violent. Many men with DID are incarcerated and undiagnosed. Women, on the other hand, are more often treated for this mental illness and end up hospitalized. The average woman with DID has fifteen alters and the average man has eight. Less than three percent of people are affected by DID.

Many people with DID were abused as children and ultimately become so detached from reality that they begin viewing their life like a television show or movie. During this state, they often go into a trance called disassociation. They can remain there indefinitely or until an alter takes over to help them live. A person may or may not remember what happens when an alter is in charge of the body.

The most common DID cases take intensive therapy to treat. While there is no cure, a combination of medications and bi-weekly therapy can often resolve the symptoms of DID in about four years. However, for more extreme cases, DID requires long-term hospitalization. About five percent of DID cases are treated in psychiatric hospitals—with these cases lasting decades when there are other mental illnesses also at play.

Alters is a work of fiction and in no way any part of any case study or based on a real client or a real client's alters. Instead, it's a made up story about one woman facing a very real condition; written in an effort to better understand.

Reader's Guide to DID Terminology

ALTER: Alternate personality that has split off or disassociated from the main personality, usually after severe childhood trauma, but not always. Also known as split, voice, alter ego, minor ego, or minor.

DISASSOCIATION: Separation of a thought process or emotion from conscious awareness. Can occur when an alter is in charge of the main personality.

PERSONALITY: Group of characteristics that motivate behavior and set us apart from other individuals.

SWITCHING or SWITCH: Process by which an alternate personality, or alter, reveals itself and controls behavior.

TRAUMA: An extremely severe emotional shock.

HOST or HALTER: The primary personality and/or body carrying around one or more personalities. Also known as main, main personality, or dominant.

7

Cheat Sheet to Lola's Alters
"And who are *you* today?"

THE HOST (Personality): Lola Murray –
Age 51, suffers from paranoid
schizophrenia and dissociative identity
disorder, formerly known as multiple
personality disorder. Hospitalized 30
years at Rosewood Hospital for Mental
Wellness. Desperately seeks to find out
who she is.

ALTER (Personality) ONE: Maria – Age
46, mother figure to the other alters.
Hopes to keep "the family" together.
Strives for peace and organization among
the alters, halters, and Host.

ALTER TWO: Tim – Age 40, father
figure to the other alters. Hopes to help
Host escape. Wishes for independence
from Host and the other alters. Serves as
the family "security expert" and jack of
all trades.

ALTER THREE: Clare – Age 35, best
friend to Host. Free spirit who enjoys
making people laugh. Loves to entertain
and refuses to be quiet.

ALTER FOUR: Zoe – Age 29, surrogate mother figure to the younger alters. A collector who thrives on drama and dreams about one day making it to the big stage. Resents Host for holding the alters hostage.

ALTER FIVE: Frog – Age 20, big brother and protector of the two youngest alters. Serves as a back-up and friend to Tim. Strives to keep other alters from emerging.

ALTER SIX: Rabbit – Age 14, the smartest and most tech savvy of the alters. Lonely and depressed, Rabbit wishes she could find a friend her own age. Goal is to one day be "a normal kid."

ALTER SEVEN: Samantha – Age 7, the youngest and happiest of the alters. Having never lived outside a host or institution, tomboy Samantha loves her alter family and wishes things would never change, despite it being "kinda smushy in here."

Table of Contents

Chapter One:
Maria

"Leave her alone. Please!"

And

"She's fifty years old. She doesn't need electric shocks. She's fine the way she is."

And

"She's done nothing wrong. It was just a joke. God knows we need some humor in this place."

And

"Hush. You're just upsetting her worse." Orderly Brown quickens his pace as he pushes a patient down the hall strapped into a wheelchair. The woman is naked, her bare shoulders exposed and only covered by a thin, white hospital blanket. His voice is as cold as the uniform he wears. "I said hush."

"Where are you—" she pauses "—taking me?" A frazzled woman with the too-early wrinkles of a thousand lifetimes skittishly pleads for answers. Heavy mascara runs down her face, which appears to be melting. "I didn't mean it. Clare told me to do it. I won't listen to her anymore. Where are you taking me? Why won't you answer me?"

A motley group doesn't miss the opportunity to appease the woman. They call "You'll be back" and "You're okay…you're okay" down the long hallway. Their voices echo like broken promises. No one believes them, including the woman herself. Lola stopped believing in promises years ago.

"She's *not* okay. *None* of us are okay." This voice is darker, closer. Lola tries to ignore it but fails.

"Why can't she get it in her head that we need to get out of here? How many more years are going to go by? She's wasting our time; our lives."

Lola can barely hear her friends' muffled comforts and concerns as the large black man in white hastens his pace. A restraint buckle clicks against a wheel as he rushes down the bleached hallway. She wishes she could turn her head but knows better than to fight against manacles. She lost her own voice years ago and lacks energy to find it now. She shivers.

The orderly mumbles as he turns the corner. He has to get out of here. He isn't sure who is more insane—the patients he works with or the doctors who order their treatments. It's only been three months.

Lola Murray shakes. *Maria? Help!*

***

Maria

"Again? Really? I'm coming. I'm coming! I'll be right there. Tell Clare to take a nap. She's caused enough trouble today. Lola, where are your clothes? Good grief. I can't take my eye off of any of you for even a second."

I don't have a lot of time to talk now. I have to help Host. I suppose she can wait though, it's not like she's going anywhere. Damn Clare got her in trouble again. Dared her to run down the hallway naked screaming her head off or something. Hilarious right? Not. Just makes them think she's even crazier. Just keeps us here even longer. And then she calls me for help. I'll do my best, like always. It's not easy being the oldest in Host's head. But I wouldn't want any other position. When you're trapped, you take any control you can get. I don't know how Samantha does it. But being born in an institution, she's never known independence. There are seven of us—five girls and two boys; or more accurately, three women, two men, and two girls. It's crowded. That's probably the only thing we all agree on.

And that we want out. Sounds simple, right? Trust me. It's not that easy.

My name is Maria. I'm forty-six years old. Host's other name is Lola. Lola is what the human alters—halters—call her. We don't like to use that because we try to stay detached. It doesn't work. I was born into Host the day a first grade teacher mistook Host for a boy. Host is what people would describe as a "girly girl." I, on the other hand, couldn't be bothered with things like fancy nails and eyeliner. Frankly? I think Host looks like a clown and smells like a brothel. But had it not been for her fascination with all things Maybelline, I may never have been born.

Host is a rare bird. They say it takes sexual or physical abuse to become a host. But we—she—can't recall any such thing. I guess I'd like to think there was something more there than someone mistaking her for a boy that caused us to become trapped in her. But maybe she's just that weak. Either way, I'm here. And I think I'm here to stay. The others couldn't do this without me. And Host? Well, she'd just be lost.

No one else will do it, so I suppose I should make a few introductions. Of course, there's me, then Tim—our security expert who's always running numbers and ridiculous escape plans through his head. Clare—don't even get me started on that one. She's trouble. You'll meet her soon enough. She can't keep her mouth shut and is the reason Host is currently strapped to a bed and being moved to a new wing of the hospital. No good comes of Clare, ever. Then there's Zoe, who is about to turn thirty and a complete drama queen, and Frog, who is twenty. He was named the day the local nature museum came in to entertain the crazies with reptiles and amphibians for show and tell. I tried to talk Host out it; naming the poor guy Frog. I don't think you need to guess who came to visit the year Rabbit was born. Or what time of year it was. Rabbit's a teenager who spends more time sulking than anyone I've ever met. And last is Samantha. She's a fun and happy one who keeps things light in here. She came around when Host was hypnotized. I'm just glad the circus wasn't in town. Imagine the name Fire-eater?

Host will be drugged out of her mind for days before they move her. I hate to say it, but sometimes it's nice when she's out. It's like a sleeping baby. You never want to wake Host. At the same time, you miss her while she's gone. Or something like that.

While I have a chance, I want to tell you a little about me. Like I was saying, I came around when Host was in the first grade. A sad little thing. She got head lice the summer before school. Her momma—another one I don't like talking about—shaved her head bald. So, on the first day, she looked more like a Lloyd than a Lola. The kids laughed at her and the teacher called her a boy. She'd been picked to be the line leader—something that's usually a privilege. But when the teacher called her to task, she said, "Everyone follow this little boy, what's your name again?" Host was devastated. The kids laughed and she didn't speak for the rest of the day—the year really.

Halters can be very insensitive. I've seen them hurt Host time and time again. But like I said, Host is a little overly sensitive too. I'm not sure exactly what caused it. Host didn't have many friends—just a few boys in the neighborhood. But even they mocked her. Older boys getting her to play touch football on the shirtless team. I tried to talk her out of that. But she didn't listen to me any better back then than she does now. Heck, even less then.

For years, Host thought of me as annoying. She figured, I guess, she didn't need two mothers. And even though she's technically older than me, that's how I always felt—like her surrogate mother. There was a period where she didn't trust me at all. She had awful paranoia. Just awful. Poor thing. She's better now, but not totally. Now, with all the other alters she's got going, I'm like Michelle Duggar, constantly trying to rally the crew together and keep things in check. I think we all know what a great job Michelle Duggar did taking care of things—good grief.

Sometimes I take it too far. I admit that. It makes me nervous watching Host try to do things for herself. It wasn't her who fought off the bullies her whole childhood. That was me and Tim. It wasn't her who graduated high school with high honors. That was me, writing those English narrative essays. So now, when she gets lucid or becomes feisty, I have to try really hard to stay quiet and let her live her own life.

The thing about being an alter is you don't really have your own life. I'm okay with helping Host live hers, but sometimes it gets old being stuck in another person's body. Spending all our time in a mental hospital doesn't help the feeling of being trapped. I get frustrated that Host doesn't seem motivated to get us out of here so we can live a real life—or as close to one as possible for a bunch of alters like us. At the same time? I'm not sure I could handle the worry that would come along with watching Host try to cross a road or drive a car. We may be safer inside. Even if it means we are locked up forever.

Oh, before I forget, there's something I want to explain, in case it's not clear. Not everyone knows about these types of things, so you may not have guessed it just yet. But Host has been diagnosed with Dissociative Identity Disorder—DID. We alters refuse to see it that way, or call it that. Back in the 90s, the halter doctors called it Multiple Personality Disorder, MPD. Those were the good old days. With that diagnosis, doctors believed alters were born and brought into a person's consciousness—or something like that. Tim explains it best. Anyway, because halter doctors like to feel important, they changed it to DID—saying we weren't born, like we never existed and don't exist as people separate from Host. I wish they could visit, just for a day, so they could see how wrong they really are. I'm in here— we're in here—and I can assure you we do exist. Call it what you want, but we alters are here for a reason, our own people, and here to stay.

***

September 8, 1969

Lola

I was excited for the first day of school, a week to the day after Labor Day that year. For months, I thought about what it would like to be out of the kindergarten hallway and finally able to ride the bus with the big kids. But that was back in June. It was August, I think, when my head started itching. I tried not to tell Mom about it. She freaks out about the little things. But eventually there was nothing I could do. I just couldn't stop itching.

When she shaved my long brown hair, I knew I was in big trouble. I wasn't excited for school anymore. I don't know why she shaved my head. I wish she had done what normal mothers do. I wish she'd just used that metal comb and made me wash my hair a few hundred times. But she said I screamed too much when it tangled. I guess it's the curse of naturally curly hair.

Mom said I looked good bald. I knew I looked like I had cancer. I hoped the other kids would think that was what it was. I hoped they might feel bad for me and maybe I could make some friends through sympathy. But that wasn't the case.

Mom said not having hair was like not wearing a bra. She said it was freeing. She told me that I'd be a leader and soon all the other girls in the class would be shaving their heads too. I asked to wear a dress for the first day of school. But she said feminists didn't wear dresses. I didn't know what a feminist was and I wasn't sure I wanted to be one. She said I would understand someday. She said I'd burn my bra.

I went to school in an old tee-shirt she said was extra special because she dyed it in Rit dye. It was blue and ugly. I tried not to complain. She seemed to think it was the perfect shirt to "make a statement, Dragonfly." I didn't want to make a statement. I wanted a wig.

School started on a Monday. I didn't sleep the whole weekend before. I just stared at that ugly shirt, knowing she wouldn't let me decide on an outfit for myself. I'd rather have worn anything. I tried to hide on the bus and didn't look up as I walked to the back. I sat alone. I heard the kids snickering and laughing at me. It wasn't fun. It wasn't what I'd been looking forward to. I wasn't making a statement and I knew no other girls would ever consider shaving their heads to be like me. Mom was crazy.

If Mom hadn't been so interested in going out to see *Butch Cassidy and the Sundance Kid* or spending time with my new step-sister and father, she may have second guessed herself on the shaving my head thing. My sister's head wasn't shaved. Her hair was straight and easier to get the lice comb through. But she had lice too.

Maria tells it right. I was picked to be the line leader. The last thing I wanted to be was the leader of anything with my bald head. There was a girl in line singing *Sugar, Sugar* by The Archies. She wouldn't shut up. But she was pretty and had long blonde hair. I wanted to be her friend. I tried to sing along. Our teacher wanted us to be quiet. I just wanted to fit in. If I had shut my mouth and not sung along, none of this may have ever happened.

My heart stopped and things went blank after the teacher called me—"this little boy"—to the front of the line. I knew my outfit was bad, that ratty tee shirt topped off with bell bottoms and sneakers. But it never occurred to me that I looked like a boy. I suddenly understood why the girl with the blonde hair had twice referred to me as "icky." I'd thought it was my singing. I remember the laughing. I remember the names. I remember a few kids saying, "that's a girl!" I remember not knowing what to do or say. I remember needing Mom but hating her at the very same time. If Maria hasn't come along to save me that day, I'm not sure what would have happened. I still can't remember how she did it. I have major memory gaps. But they say that's common for people with my condition. And maybe one of the reasons that Maria and I get along so well is that we are both Virgos. We understand each other. We think the same way. She's just a heck of a lot braver than I am or ever will be. That's what Zoe would say, anyway. But Zoe's a Capricorn. And apparently, that's supposed to mean that Maria, Clare, and I get along with her just fine. So I'm not sure I believe in that horoscope stuff anyway. It's hard to know what you believe in with this many people inside you. It's never really quiet in my— our—head.

Chapter Two:
Tim

Lola can't take it any longer. *I need to at least* try *to get cleaned up. This is disgusting. And where* is *everyone?* She rises from her twin bed in the far right corner of the room she now shares with a new girl with pink hair. She can't remember the girl's name. *It doesn't matter. She won't be here long. They never stick around. Only alters stay.* Lola shrugs and walks to the shared bathroom, wishing the cold tile on the floors could be replaced with something a little warmer. *Maybe Zoe can find a rug.*

As she approaches the bathroom, she makes sure not to let the mirror catch her reflection before she's ready. There are just some things she needs to be able to control. This, she decides, will be one of them. Breathing in deep, Lola positions her body so she can edge up on the reflective paper staff feel is safer instead of a glass mirror. In its gritty reflection, she sees a face she doesn't recognize.

While the woman staring back at her is pretty enough, she isn't how Lola views herself. She hopes she's just being overly critical of her features because of the unflattering hospital lighting. *I'm too young to be gray! Where is my makeup? When will they give it back? Maybe Tim can get it back for me.* She glares at the deep crow's feet at the corners of her eyes. While she can see herself in these eyes, she's perplexed. *How did I get this old? This doesn't feel right.*

Terror—a familiar feeling—grips Lola's chest as she sinks to the cramped bathroom floor. *Tim will say no. Maria will yell at me. They won't care how I look. They only care about practical things.* She holds her knees to her chest and bows her head, wondering if it's the upgraded dose of Risperdal Dr. Hillcrest ordered that is making her fuzzy. *Maria's right. Stop letting Clare control you. She only gets you in trouble and you lose your makeup. At least Clare cares about makeup. Clare has style.*

Her thoughts are interrupted by the door to her room—room 262—opening adjacent to the bathroom. Light footsteps follow with a 'plop' onto the bed across the room from hers. She knows it must be her new roommate and wishes the girl would go away. Then she reconsiders. *Maybe Rabbit could finally have a friend. That would be nice.* Lola peeks around the corner, careful to be sure the new

24

roommate doesn't see her just yet. In her early twenties, the girl seems to care more about listening to her iPod than making any attempt toward mental wellness. *Stand up. Maria will get mad if you just sit here feeling sorry for yourself.* Lola rises and washes her face in the sink without looking at the reflective paper again. *Maybe I can borrow makeup from her or at least introduce her to Rabbit.*

Back in the room, the strange girl's body language shows a reckless, childish nature that is anything but childlike. Even her posture is resistant to rules; slumped and strong all at the same time. Clare might like her too. Whether the body language is the truth or just an act, Lola can't be sure. The girl is thin, but not unhealthily so. Her rosy hair hangs low over her shoulders and down her back with a purple streak that starts at her temples and follows her hair through its twisty strands. Her head bobs up and down, acknowledging Lola's presence. But she doesn't remove her ear buds. Hip hop music Lola is unfamiliar with blares from the girl's ears and she is thankful she won't have to make small talk. There will be plenty of time to introduce her new roommate to Rabbit and Clare later. *They will like her best. For different reasons, of course, but that doesn't really matter. At least they won't fight.*

Lola sits on the edge of her bed and calls Maria with her mind to ask her what to do next. Three days of being restrained and heavily medicated from the latest Clare incident has her unsure of how she will navigate her move to a new wing in the mental unit. The last time she talked to any of the alters she was being pushed down the hall of the crisis wing. She swallows and tries to put the memory out of her mind. For months now, the alters have begged her to do whatever she needs to get them all out of Rosewood. But asking to be discharged and taking the steps to do it are two different things. If they want it bad enough, Lola decides, they can do it themselves. And Lola's not sure she'd even know how to survive on the outside. *Maria? Clare? Zoe? Where are you guys? I need help here. Can any of you take this on for me?*

***

Tim

"No! Stay out of it! Do you *really* think she needs more distractions? No more switching or crosstalk today. Go find something else to do—geesh. Now, get out of here. I'm trying to think."

Maria moans that being the oldest is hardest. Don't listen to her. I never listen to her when she starts with the whining shit. She likes to hear herself speak. Maybe if she had done a better job micro-managing things, there would be more space in here. You want to talk problems? Try being a man trapped in a woman's body. Better, a crazy woman's body. Let's just say I spend a lot of time by myself. I try to avoid the drama. I don't say much and only come out when I have to. Host never really talks about me, or with me, for that matter. It's probably because she doesn't want anyone to know there are guys in here. Host likes to think she's a feminist but we're the first one she calls when trouble comes. And only then. Sometimes, I pretend I don't hear her. Any of them.

I think of myself as a security guard. I first arrived in 1975, the day Host got beat up by a boy for trying to defend her friend at the bus stop. I don't like men or boys who beat up on girls. Let me tell you, I slugged him one and he never messed with Host again. That kind of drama I don't mind; when it involves fists and making things right. I'm a protector, like Frog. We guys gotta stick together. It's like an estrogen factory in here.

It's too crowded, living in Host. I've done the math. I'm great with numbers. If you take a 160 pound, 5 foot 8 grown woman and you use a little geometry, it's not hard to realize that there are seven of us—eight if you count Host— living in a 7.56 square foot area. I know tiny houses are all the rage right now, but really? You try dealing with that many women in one spot.

The best way I can explain this living situation is to think of Host's body as a tiny house. We each have our own room in her brain and do most of our living in other parts of her body. Frog and me have our man's cave in the basement; me in the medulla oblongata—ground control—him in the cerebellum, making sure we keep balance. Sam—Samantha—has a room here too. I'm not sure if it's because she's a tomboy or because she gravitates to the pons, which controls the brain's subconscious thought. It makes sense, I guess. She was born through hypnosis— the result of Host not paying attention. Typical woman. Probably worried about her makeup.

Then you have the mother hens controlling the house and living on the main floor micro-managing everything. We guys learn to stay away from them. If that sounds sexist, as I've been told, I can't really say I'm sorry. I only speak the truth. Maria's room is the hypothalamus— where she makes sure everything runs smoothly. Zoe lives in the amygdala, queen of strong emotions and her biggest excuse for the drama. Whatever. Samantha often sleeps with her. God help us all in ten years if any of that drama rubs off.

Rabbit and Clare have the attic; Rabbit to the left, Clare to the right. I try not to go up there, unless it's for repairs or I need to speak with a halter. When we alters talk to the halters, we do it from the front lobby— Host's frontal lobe. And lately, Clare seems to be moving into the frontal lobe. If you knew Clare, you'd understand why that isn't helping matters. Talk about a cat fight waiting to happen.

As for Host, she's been hanging out in the hippocampus, near Maria. But I doubt it will last. They tend to get on each other's nerves after a bit. It's like a mother-daughter relationship. Eventually, she'll go back to Zoe's couch near the heart. If she can find it—Zoe's a hoarder.

During the day, we try to spread things out a bit. I think we'd kill each other if we didn't. If you think seven square feet of an entire house is small, try sharing one brain. It isn't easy, the life of an alter. Mostly, I wish I could escape out the tips of Host's toes. But I try not to complain.

The only time I really get involved is when it's time for a meeting. We alters meet up every week or so to figure out a way to get Host to get out of here. As long as she's stuck in a psych ward, we are too. Then, there's always how to get out of Host to consider, but that's a long way off. I'm a realist. I don't like to think about things that are too far in the future. And, the truth is that chances are, we'll never get out.

Maria is saying I have to tell you more about me. Micromanagement at its finest. I don't want to listen to her nag, so I will do my best. If I can get my story out she may focus more on the real work at hand: Getting us out. Without Maria, the other alters won't do anything. Even with her, there will be a fight. She and I butt heads a lot but we've learned, after all these years, to try to work together. I think of us as the co-parents—never married, thank God—to the other five and to Host. But I'm no father to Host. I just want to make that clear. Maria thinks she's Host's mother or something. It's obnoxious.

Like I was saying, I came around the day Host got in a fight. Micro-managing Maria was sleeping—Don't give me that look, Maria, let me talk and tell it my way or I'm going to shut up and go back to my planning. Anyway, who knew a simple nap could be enough to create a whole new life? Someone had to help Host. Ever since, I'm always the first to help when Host finds herself in trouble. Just yesterday, when she got herself into more trouble, I had to go with Maria to calm her down. Of course, I won't get thanked for it. Only Maria gets and takes the credit. It's fine. I don't need a thank you note. What I need? *All* I need? Is to get out.

Getting out isn't going to be as easy as it sounds. I've tried for forty years. Host won't let us go. She thinks of us as her best friends. I've done all the research. Host isn't your average multiple personality disorder Host. The halters have diagnosed her with schizophrenia, paranoid type too. Took the stupid halters more than a decade to figure that out. I could have told 'em that without the fancy education. Those first few years were rough. Before she became medicated, she believed Maria and I were out to get her too. The only one she trusted was Clare, which is really a total joke. Clare is the one who hurts her, if anything. But what do I know? No one listens to me. I'm glad that's calmed down at least. She trusts us now. The down side is that now she trusts us *too* much and won't live her own life—or at least pretend to so we can finally be free.

I don't know what else Maria wants me to say. It's not like I have a life. My life is about helping Host escape or get discharged. I have figured out ten escape plans. Every time I present them to the group, the girls look at me like I'm crazy. Only Frog's game. It's frustrating. I wish we could have a guys' day where we shut the women down and take over for Host. That would mean progress. That would set us free. I'm just not sure what we'd do next—another area where Maria and I agree. And that doesn't happen much. Okay, I'm out of here. I'm tired of Maria's dirty looks.

***

November 16, 1975

Lola

It wasn't even a school day when Tim first came around. Instead, the fight broke out in our neighborhood, oddly, at the bus stop. I'm not sure what we were even doing there. It was a Sunday, or maybe a Saturday. But I think a Sunday. I know we went to church that morning.

Back in 1975, there weren't a lot of things you did to entertain yourself. I often got sick of playing with my step-sister, Charlotte. I'm not sure why. Maybe it's because she could do no wrong. Maybe it's because I felt like I was forced to be her friend. Either way, she was one of my only true friends. I probably should have appreciated her more. Friends aren't easy for me to find or keep. Maybe that's part of my mental issues too. I can't really be sure. At least I'm able to be friendly with the alters. That counts for something, right? Or maybe it's that I don't really need friends with all my "imaginary ones." I hate that term.

Anyway, a group of us from the neighborhood were out playing in the snow. Snow had come early that year. I think even by Halloween. I was about twelve. Maria hates the cold and hates playing outside and had decided to take a nap. Back then, I was in charge most of the time. Maria only really came out when I ran into problems. But with her sleeping, she didn't see or hear about this one kid—Travis—picking on my friend Wendy with

33

buck teeth and wild orange hair. He wouldn't stop. Instead of building snowmen with the rest of us, he kept taunting her, singing "Here come's Wendy, floatin' down the Delaware, chewin' on her underwear, can't afford another pair." I'm not sure what made me do it, but I snapped. Wendy was a tiny thing. A few years younger too, maybe ten? Anyway, when he grabbed her brand new orthodontic retainer, I lost it. I chased him into a snowbank. But before I knew it he was giving me a white wash and his teasing and attention turned to me.

I can't remember meeting Tim or feeling him be born. He was the fastest to show up. And it scared me that he was a boy. But I was glad to have him. I'll never forget the look on Travis's face. And he never messed with either me or Wendy again. Tim doesn't realize it, but he was my hero that day. I'd love to tell him that, but I'm not sure how. He's been my hero since, for the most part. There have been exceptions. He isn't perfect. None of us are. He looks out for us like a father, but he says he doesn't want to be anyone's father. He says if he were a main personality, or a halter, as they like to call us hosts, he'd never have kids. Instead, he'd live off the land in the wilderness to

34

"never be bothered with women again." I guess I can't blame him. I know he's not happy inside of me. I wish there was something I could do about that but I can't imagine what it would be like to not have him ready to protect me no matter what. I guess I can be pretty selfish.

Chapter Three:
Clare

Lola begins her walk of shame down a wide corridor with a well-liked orderly named Paul. He's the only orderly at Rosewood who allows patients to call him by his first name. It's only been a few days since her most feisty of alters dared her to cause a scene in a similar hallway. That stunt got her restrained and her meds increased but Paul's been nice enough not to bring it up. Now, feeling a little more lucid, it makes her laugh that the hospital staff feels she still needs an usher to see her psychiatrist after thirty years. *At least it's only Paul. Maybe this is something Clare could use in her stand-up routine for the next talent night. I'll have to tell her that,* Lola thinks. The hallway is a long, almost non-descript white; a mock passage to heaven. However, the hustle and bustle of mental hospital life still makes Lola feel odd, even after all these years. *I'm like Jack Nicholson in* One Flew Over The Cuckoo's Nest.

Paul knocks on Dr. Hillcrest's door.

"Lola Murray here for you," he calls out to the dark wood.

"Come on in!" Dr. Hillcrest sings.

He's in a good mood. Good. Despite his happy tone, Lola wishes she could disappear.

"Hi, Lola. Good to see you. I heard you were feeling better today." Dr. Hillcrest smiles from behind his desk as he rises to meet her. His desk is tidy. She doesn't know why she thought it would be messier. She's seen it before. She knows he's a neat freak—opposite of alter Zoe.

Lola feels like a six-year-old, wondering whose making reports to him on her progress now. She tells herself she should be used to it and tries to remember which alter met with the psychiatrist last time. She can't remember.

"Yes, thanks," she says.

"I'm off. Buzz me when you're all set," Paul says to Dr. Hillcrest, nodding at Lola.

Lola reminds herself to make eye contact like Maria told her to and not look at the ground.

"Have a seat, Lola," Dr. Hillcrest says, motioning to the leather couch in his posh office. "How have things been?"

The PhD diploma on the far wall catches her attention. Theodore Hillcrest. The name seems strange to her somehow; like it is just another foreign thing in this surreal world that is supposed to be tangible. *You need to start showing up for your own appointments more often. Stop letting the alters handle your business,* Lola tells herself, ignoring the alters' background chit chat in her brain. The doctor's office is a major contrast to the hallway; there are bookcases of books that range from therapy to poetry and even a few bean bag chairs in the far corner by the large leather couch. *Zoe would like it in here if she could mess it up a little.* Lola wonders how she, herself, feels about this place. But she's never been good at having her own opinion—on anything. It makes her angry that she knows she's been here before but can't quite remember anything but his desk—the curse of sharing one mind with seven others.

Lola is cautious at first. "Good. I mean, I'm a little confused but I think it's just the meds. I'm having some trouble making sense of things. I know I had an—urrr—outburst. That was Clare's fault. But I'm fine now. Can we decrease the dose? Everything seems foggy."

Dr. Hillcrest nods. "All these things are normal for your diagnosis, Lola. Go on."

Lola—*Tim and Frog more likely*—wants to hit him. The righteous look on his face makes her want to tear into him about how he doesn't have a clue what's normal for her. But Lola refrains. *Play this cool. Listen to Maria. She's in charge.*

"So I guess I'm just working on making sense of things," she says, throwing the doctor's perceived know-it-all tone back at him.

"Okay then. That's a great place to start!"

Lola wants to vomit at how patronizing his voice sounds. It takes all she has not to allow her disgust to show in her face. *Play this right and you'll get your makeup back, Maria said so.* But she can't keep the frown from spreading across her face. Much to her annoyance, Dr. Hillcrest meets her frown with a gentle smile of empathy as he returns to business, picking up his clipboard and leaning back into his rolling desk chair.

"What would you like to focus on today? It's not often I talk to the *real* Lola versus your other versions of Lola," he continues. "I'm hoping that you'll be able to stay with us this time so we can make more progress than in the past."

"How long was I with you last time?" Lola asks, more for her own information than any intention of having a conversation with the doctor.

"About two hours. Four months ago," he says, his eyes softening.

"Oh." Lola stares at the floor.

"It's okay. Maria's been around; we're friends too, Lola. I think this new drug combination seems to be working. Sometimes it just takes a while to get the right mix. This time may be different," Dr. Hillcrest says. "We can forget about the Clare incident. I know she's a spunky one and it may just have been your body getting used to the med change."

"When can I—*don't say we*—get out of here?"

Dr. Hillcrest looks up from his clipboard and stares into Lola's chocolate eyes.

"As soon we can quiet those voices down," he says. "But you have to understand, it won't be fast. There's a lot of transitioning that will need to be done. Baby steps."

"But I don't understand what the big deal is. Even *if* the voices are fake what harm is there in letting me leave this place so I can start my life?" Lola asks, telling Zoe to shut up—that she's doing her best to negotiate with the man. "It's not like any of us have ever tried to hurt anyone. Sure, Clare can be a little outrageous. Rabbit's had her moments, but those are over now. How is that dangerous?"

"Lola, do you have any idea why you were originally hospitalized?" Dr. Hillcrest asks.

Lola shrugs. *Because no one believes that my voices are real people.*

"I don't think it's a good idea to get into all of that yet," Dr. Hillcrest says. "I was thinking it might be better to start a little more slowly now that we have you—not your alters—back with us."

Dr. Hillcrest reaches into the open filing cabinet behind him and pulls out a stack of papers and envelopes in a six-inch thick binder. He tries—unsuccessfully—to make sure it doesn't spill onto his otherwise immaculate desk.

Lola recognizes the handwriting on the envelopes that leaks from the binder. She knows, instantly, that the envelopes were written on by her mother—Stella Murray—and wonders why they are in Dr. Hillcrest's possession.

"Are those from my mom? Why do you…" Lola asks.

Dr. Hillcrest smiles and jots on his clipboard after digging it back out from the pile.

"I'm impressed! You recognize her handwriting. This is great, Lola!"

"Well, what is it?" Lola asks. "Why do you have those? Is she okay?"

"Yes. She's perfectly fine. Don't worry about that. Actually, Lola, they are for you. Your mother has been writing to you all these years. She's also been visiting you. She's asked me to keep them for you until a day like today where you would recognize them and understand why and what—"

"Those are all letters?" Lola interrupts, aware of how great her mother was at writing to her when she went to summer camp as a child. "Can I have them?" *Why didn't Maria tell me mother has been visiting and writing all these years? I'm going to kill her!*

"Yes, I'm going to send them back to your room with you to read between the next few sessions and possibly to share in the group," Dr. Hillcrest says. "But first there are a few things you need to know."

Lola nods, knowing better than to try to protest. She doesn't want to lose what could be the key to understanding her current predicament or the safety in Stella's words.

"I'm not sure if you're ready to hear everything but I'm going to start with what I feel you can handle and if it's too much I need you to tell me, okay?" Dr. Hillcrest asks, his eyes burning into Lola's forehead. "It's so important that you tell me immediately so you don't go back inside yourself and let the alters take over again."

"I understand. Is that what happened last time?" Lola asks.

"Yes."

"Okay. I understand. I promise," Lola pledges.

"Let's review some of the things the mental health workers have told you about so far. For starters, you came to the state hospital in 1984. At the time, you were in college and had experienced some trauma. And of course, there was the trauma from high school too. I don't want to get into the details of that just yet. How is this feeling so far?" Dr. Hillcrest interrupts himself.

"I'm fine. I promise not to interrupt unless I can't handle what you tell me. Please go on," Lola begs. "If you're asking me to trust you with how much you tell me, I need you to trust me with how much I can handle." *Maria's already told me everything anyway, jerk. Well, then again, she didn't tell me about Mom.*

"Okay, fair enough." Dr. Hillcrest laughs.

"So when you were first hospitalized you were in your early twenties. You were at the state hospital for well over a decade and a half and stuck inside yourself. There

43

were, three? Maybe four voices—alters—that we knew about at the time," Dr. Hillcrest explains. "Since then, we've met more. But many are new."

Lola smiles, encouraging him to continue.

"Okay. So my point is that you invented this world to escape reality. It was easier to let your alters deal with your problems. Does that make sense?"

"I think I understand, I've learned enough in my groups about my illness, but I'm curious about how we're supposed to fix this?" Lola asks.

"Well, Lola. That's something I think we can work on deciding together. First, I want to see how you handle these letters and what's inside them. I think it's going to take some time to establish where you're at and come up with a new treatment plan. I'm going to need to keep meeting with Lola—not Maria, not Clare—do you understand?"

Lola nods. "I understand. Do you think I could get my make-up back?"

***

Clare

"Did someone say makeup? And Doc? You can't shut me up. Not on your life! Maria? Maybe and good luck. But I was born to entertain, Girl! Hey, great timing on the makeup. You rock! We'll be stunning again in no time. Ya proud of me for keepin' Maria distracted?"

I love Host. I don't know what the others complain about. Sure, she's messed up. But who ain't? Sometimes I get jealous of her. I wish I was Host. I'd do things different. But what girl doesn't sometimes get jealous of her BFF?

Personally? I think Host is doin' the best she can. I mean, you try to live in a mental ward with a group of psychos whose idea of a good time is art therapy. How many self-portraits can a girl make without wanting to mix things up a bit? So, she colors outside the lines sometimes. And? When Host draws me, it's always in bright colors. Ya can't throw me in a brown dress, girlfriend. And even if ya do, I'll still steal the show.

That's the one thing I don't like about Host, ya'll. She doesn't always take the greatest care of our body and sometimes I have to spend weeks working off the vending machine Twinkies she eats endlessly. Between her and Sam, we're never gonna keep a decent figure for long.

And let me tell ya, Host's not all that grateful that I keep her together as nicely as I do. But I guess that's just the sort of thing ya do for friends. BFFs anyway.

I arrived on Host's sixteenth birthday—fashionably late. Sweet one-six, baby. Sixteen and never been kissed. That was Host. Host's best human—halter—friend had just gotten her driver's license. Host was pissed that her parents wouldn't let her get her license too. They weren't supposed to go to the mall. But like I told ya'll, Host can be a lot of fun, and ignored the rules. I guess I'm supposed to be sad that her best friend died that day in an accident on the highway. But I like to think that maybe that's why I'm here. Maybe I'm her best friend reincarnated. Holly was a lot of fun from what I've heard. Died tryin' to find the perfect song to groove to. Pat Benatar I think it was—woman after my own heart. Anyway, I can't really talk right now. Gotta scoot. Host can't do her makeup without me. If I leave her to herself, she'll look like the love child of Tammy Faye and Bozo. We can't be having that. Talent show's comin' up. Chow for now!

***

September 12, 1979

Lola

I just wanted an ordinary birthday. I was pissed that Mom and Travis wouldn't let me get my license. Mom said there was plenty of time for that, changing the rules without warning me. "Driving isn't necessary, Dragonfly," she'd said. She told me not to rush my childhood. I remember wondering where all her talk of freedom and feminism went: *Had our new step family really changed her that much? What would she think now if I burned my bra?* I felt like she was being selfish. But my best friend, Holly? Well, her parents were cool. And she had her license. Brand new, warm plastic. And we wanted to celebrate. But that day turned out to be anything but ordinary. There really isn't a word for what it turned out to be.

Holly was my first real friend in high school. By then, Wendy had moved from the neighborhood and I kept to myself mostly. I can't talk about what happened that day. But Clare has a theory. She believes in reincarnation. She believes that when Holly died on our way to the mall, she—Clare—showed up inside of me as

Holly so we would never have to leave each other.

Only a week before she died, Holly and I had pledged to be BFFs forever. We'd cut our wrists and become blood sisters. It was something better than what me and "be-nice-she's-your-sister-now" Charlotte would ever have.

Holly understood me. She wasn't afraid of Tim or Maria. In fact, she liked them. She said they were like the adoptive parents we should have had, instead of her druggie parents and my over-protective and contradictory mother. We wished we were real sisters and that Maria and Tim were our real parents. But what I never told Holly was that, back then, I wasn't so sure I really trusted Tim and Maria. Sure, they'd saved me. But they were bossy too. And sometimes, when they took over or Maria caused conflict with Mom, I wasn't so sure I was that lucky to have them living inside me. It was complicated. Holly didn't need to hear it. She had real problems, like an alcoholic father and a mother who was into LSD.

Clare remembers most of what happened that day. The only thing I know she's wrong about is that she thinks Holly and I were listening to Pat Benatar. I don't know where she gets it. The songs we were fighting over on the radio were *We Don't Talk Anymore* by Cliff Travis and *My Sharona* by The Knack. I still can't hear *My Sharona* without an instant anxiety attack. Luckily, Clare lost that eight-track a month after Holly died anyway. By then, I was too far gone to pay attention anyway. And really, why does it even matter? Holly is gone and never will be back, no matter who Clare thinks she is.

Sometimes, I get nervous around Clare because she knows what I did. It was Holly's idea. But I was the one who did it. I should have said no. But I've never been good about saying no. It's probably why I can't say no to Clare when she gives me a dare. What if she told? What if the others knew? What would they think of me? I know the older ones know. But they don't bring it up. Clare might kill them. They won't admit it, but they're afraid of her. They think she's crazy. I think she might be too, but I'm not exactly in a position to judge now, am I?

What is great about Clare, though, is she really is my best friend now. We fight sometimes, but she's great for doing all the things I used to do with Holly. She's the first and only alter that I've trusted since the very moment she arrived. And she's probably the one I should trust the least, according to the others. But she's fun. She takes my mind off of things like being locked up in a mental hospital, for starters. And she makes me laugh. All the time. We like to do makeup together. Either I get out of the way and let her be in charge or she gives me instructions as I put it on myself. She does a better job than me, but it's fun to have her around; like having a best friend there for company as you get ready for a date or something.

I've never gotten ready for a real date. I've never had a relationship. Who would want me? And Frog and Tim? Well, they wouldn't tolerate it. They've made it clear, they aren't gay and they can't stand the idea of kissing another man "just because you're a girl." They say it's hard to be an alter. But it's not easy being a host either. Keeping everyone happy is nearly impossible. Some days, I just give up. That's when I get quiet. Sometimes I stay that way. The doctors call it disassociation.

Chapter Four:
Zoe

I'm crazy! Lola shakes and reminds herself to shut her mouth as she reads her mother's words that evening in the safety of her tiny shared room. She's grateful her pink-haired-roomie isn't around.

She picks up another letter, stained yellow by the near thirty years it waited for her, determined to get through as many as she can before someone checks on her:

Dear Lola, April 4, 1985

We miss you so much! Your sister hasn't been the same since you left. Truthfully? None of us have. I spoke to Dr. Bergeron last week and she said you are still stuck in that stubborn head of yours. Please come out, little Dragonfly. I miss you dearly! I've decided to have her save these letters for you until you are ready.

I know what happened is not your fault. I hope you aren't still blaming yourself. I know how critical you can be. When I came to visit last week you didn't seem to know who I was. I think it's the medications. They need to think about herbal stuff. They have you so drugged out you don't recognize your own mother!

Travis and I have been in all sorts of trouble these days. We've taken composting a bit too far and now all the neighbors are using our yard as a landfill. I'm sure you'll get quite the chuckle out of that one, dear.

We're thinking of going up to Niagara Falls for the weekend but I'm not sure about missing a visit with you. Sometimes, I feel like I can just will you to come back to me and I'm so afraid to miss that one chance when you do remember my face.

I miss you so much, Lola. I'm not giving up on you. Not ever.

Love Always,

Mom

PS—Make sure they are feeding you right. No more of this starving yourself. You're beautiful!

Maybe Dr. Hillcrest has a point, Lola muses. She swallows regret for having no memory of pretty much any of the mid-eighties and early nineties. Almost all of her memories are of Rosewood and Rosewood alone. In fact, it's hard to fully comprehend life outside of Rosewood. *Maybe I don't want to know all of these things. Maybe Maria's wrong and I'm not ready for this. It's safer here.* Still, she misses her mother. *How long has it been?*

And I've never starved myself. That must have been Clare.

Lola carefully folds the letter and places it back in its envelope, then into a larger one in a binder. She tucks the binder under her bed, next to her cotton swabs, before heading to the bathroom to wash her face. She needs a break. She'll need a clear head to sort through this. At the moment? That's not happening.

***

Zoe

"Be serious! *One* letter? Come *on*! We'll be stuck in Rosewood *another* thirty years at this rate! I'll be fifty-eight, Lola. Your mother won't be *alive* by then."

I can't understand Host. Why she would be content to spend the rest of her life in this place is beyond me. Clare swears she's doing her best to get out. But I don't buy it. I think she'd stay here forever if we weren't pushing her to get us out. I get it that it's easy here. They do the cooking and most of the cleaning. We have to have our rooms tidy and all that but it's pretty easy other than that. People here are mean and give me crap for collecting things. Maybe if Host tried a little harder to get out, we'd be able to live how we want to. If I could live in the real world, I'd have collections of amazing treasures. I'd spend my weekends at flea markets. I like to find the gem in everything. But I have a hard time doing that inside Host. Maybe the gem in her is Sam. I like to pretend Sam is my kid; seeing as Host and I will never have kids of our own. Not at this rate.

I was picked up when Host was twenty-two, or was it twenty-one? Maria and Clare talk about what it's like outside of here. I wouldn't know. I was born here, somewhere between Host's straight jacket and a three-week medically induced zombie coma. If those three had been quieter, maybe I could have tasted freedom. But no one can tell Maria and Tim what to do. And Clare? You try to shut her up. She's like a drunken party girl. Pathetic for a thirty-five- year-old.

The others don't think it matters when you're born. At least when you're an alter. I couldn't disagree more. But if you've been paying attention, this won't surprise you. I was born on a Friday, under the sign of the Capricorn. Reagan was president and the hit movie at the time was *Boxcar Bertha*. I'm glad Host skipped movie night that week, Bertha would have been a horrible name. Zoe just fits me. They say Capricorns are practical, prudent, and ambitious. They say we are pessimistic and fatalistic, miserly and grudging. Well, I've worked hard to break past those things and work harder to be more like a Taurus. If Host could have held on for a few more days, I could have been born under a sign more reflective of who I am. That would save a lot of arguments with Frog, but Frog likes to argue anyway, so I guess it's okay.

I can be pessimistic. I'll admit that. It's not that I see the glass as half empty. I know the glass is refillable. The problem is that it's hard to be optimistic when you have no control over your own life, or even body. Can you imagine what it's like to not have your own body? Sometimes, I'm with Clare and think alters are the reincarnated, doing purgatory for a bad last life. Maybe this is our punishment, or there's a lesson to learn, being trapped like this. I'm not sure. It's something I like to talk to Frog about on good days. But lately, I haven't had a lot of good days.

Back to the point; my birthday, and even better, me! I came around when Host was around twenty-one. She was just finishing up college. Never did get that degree, poor thing. Had I come around earlier, like Maria and Tim and Clare, I'd know what it was like to live outside a nuthouse. But I'm making the best of it. I watch a lot of television and hope to one day be a soap opera actress, or better yet, a Broadway star. That must have been what I was in my last life. Maybe I was so good and so famous that I had to come back trapped in Host in order to be humbled. Waste of talent if you ask me.

Many things are wasted around here. People don't see that things can have many uses. For example, every week, after art therapy, the therapists throw away all the scrap construction paper. Not me. I go back and find uses for it. It usually gets me in trouble. But I don't see why things need to be thrown away. I've been permanently banned from the recycling bin. I'm okay with that now, because I know at least with recycling, it's being put to another use. Then again, I'm not sure why I care about the environment. It's not like we get outside much. What does weather matter when you're locked in a stuffy hospital most of the day? Most of our "outside" time is in an atrium, which isn't outside at all. Sorry if I'm repeating myself. It's always hard to think with Clare around.

But Clare isn't *all* bad. I *love* when she performs. It's really Host I have the problem with. If I could get out of here, I'd be on Broadway. When Clare does her stand-up routines for the halters I get excited. She really is a funny one. I wish I could collect her jokes the way I collect other things.

In my free time, when I'm not hanging out with Sam or Rabbit, I like to write screenplays. I find treasures around the hospital and use them to create a story. Just another example of how collecting and recycling can be fun. Someday, I hope to have a one-man show. I may steal some of Clare's material. But don't tell her.

**

January 18, 1985

Lola

Zoe showed up not long before or after I was first admitted into Rosewood. None of us are quite clear on this and I'm not sure it matters. I just know I was under hypnosis that day. So, I suppose it had to be before I arrived. Or, it could have been when I was in therapy before being admitted. I saw a lot of shrinks back then. I was trying to prevent a meltdown: Epic fail.

I'm not sure what caused me to melt down. I was wrapping up college. I thought I had everything under control. It was my last semester. I was taking more classes than I probably should have and really stressed out about what kind of job I should be getting. What does a person with a sociology degree *do*, exactly? The idea of moving back in with Mom wasn't my favorite. And trying to study for finals before Christmas the prior semester had me on edge. I remember playing my Chicago record over and over and wishing I could just be done and have my degree in hand. I'm not sure what I planned to do with it.

Having lived with alters inside of me so long, I grew up secretly feeling like there was no way I could ever survive as a normal adult. And maybe that's what made me snap. Keeping my separate worlds secret for more than a decade. Secrets can do that, you know—cause a person to snap. We learned that in group therapy. Or, it could have been the idea of adulthood in general. I knew I couldn't let Maria live my life for me. But look at me now. I can't even decide when to eat or what time to go to bed. Instead, for the last God knows how many years, I have hospital staff doing it for me. Maybe I should have majored in how to be a professional nuthouse patient.

Believe it or not, I had a 4.0 grade point average. I prided myself on getting better grades in school than my step-sister Charlotte. I knew my mother wished I was more like Charlotte. But it was something Mom could brag about—"Lola gets the best grades! I never have to worry about her." I hate when people worry about me. Then again, at least it shows they care.

It's all quite disappointing. I wonder, sometimes, what my family really thinks of me. From what I hear, they still love me and care about me but I wouldn't really know that first hand. When I think about ever going back—something the alters want more than anything—I feel exactly like I did that last semester in college; terrified.

Zoe likes to tell me that it would all have worked out had I only met a man. The thing is, you don't really seek out relationships when you know your partner would have to share you with multiple people. Back then, having alters wasn't something I exactly advertised. Instead, I went to class, worked a part time job at a fast food joint, and went back to class. I figured the less people that knew me or got near me, the better off we would all be. Besides, Maria gets jealous.

Zoe says all I had to do was find myself a good Capricorn or Taurus. I wish it was that easy. But I'm not sure I'd even want to do that to anyone, let alone have children—another of her goals. Once, we had a psychic come in to Rosewood. Zoe insisted on being in charge that day and let the psychic do Tarot card and palm readings. The woman, who didn't look particularly psychic to me—but what would that look like?—insisted my palm lifeline said I would have four children. I might have believed her had she said seven; one for each of the alters living inside me now. But who knows, there could be more coming. They always come. And you can't tie your tubes when it comes to alters. They are just born. All you can do is love them and hope they get along with the others.

As for me? I don't think I could have saved myself. My big mistake wasn't avoiding meeting a Capricorn prince charming. My big mistake was being so overtired and stressed out that I forgot to refill my meds. By then, Mom wasn't paying attention anymore. She thought it was just another phase. I really should have known better. But my prescription was at school and I was staying with Mom over break. Living with Mom is enough to stress anyone out. It's another reason I'm not sure I want to leave here. I guess I go back and forth on it. But I also don't think that's *up* to me now, not if the alters have anything to say about it. They are pretty determined that, one way or another, we are leaving Rosewood forever and soon. If I ever do get out, I am going to have to be religious about when and how I take my meds. I really don't want to do this all over again. And I can't imagine how many more will show up if I do take a nuthouse 2.0 tour. Gross.

Chapter Five:

Frog

Maybe the Jell-O's not so bad. Frog likes it. But Frog eats anything. Clare would freak.

Lola sits across from Justin and Edna the next day in the hospital dining hall at lunch. They play with their orange Jell-O. Lola can't stop watching them but tries not to be obvious about it. It's strange being in a new wing, but it's not a bad thing, either. It's a sign she might get out of here someday. The floors are made of white tile and all of the tables are long with dark blue plastic stools attached. There are eight stools to a table. The serving lines are still full as the rest of the lower classified patients wait their turns in a buffet style lunch line. The less lucid patients eat on their floors with far less choices—like Lola did for so many years. Lola is glad to move around more freely than some of the other, worse-off residents. In less than a half hour, combined with the brief time they'd spent together that morning at breakfast, Lola has surmised the following of her new dining companions:

Justin is a twenty-year-old with Down Syndrome and rage issues. If she had to diagnose him quickly, her best guess would be Intermittent Explosive Disorder. She hasn't gotten a diagnosis wrong in ten years. A person picks up on these things living in a mental health unit. Orderly Paul has filled her in on how Justin often throws things in the dining hall when he doesn't like what's being served and warned Lola not to sit directly across from him. But Lola likes to think she is both curious and a risk taker. *Just like Clare.*

Justin came to Rosewood about two years ago. Having moved out of his family home at eighteen, Justin had a year of independence with workers coming to check on him and drive him to appointments. But after quitting his job as a bagger at the local supermarket, Justin had become bored and frustrated and caused one too many scenes in local bars where he was convinced he could find a girlfriend.

His IQ is higher than most with Down Syndrome and he knows enough to know he is different. This is a major source of frustration for a young man who is interested in meeting a girl and curious about the opposite sex. Lola feels bad for him and likes him instantly. She wonders

63

what Frog will think of him. His brown hair is unkempt—*Frog won't like that*—and she has an urge to get a comb and do his hair properly since he doesn't seem to care to do it himself. *Clare could help him.* Justin hopes to be released soon to return to his foster mother's care and "finally get a girlfriend with pink hair."

Next to Justin sits Edna. Edna is a sixty-eight-year-old woman who has bounced from hospital to hospital since she was middle-aged. Having spent thirty years institutionalized, Edna doesn't make any bones about being sick of her situation. At the same time, Lola senses that she's accepted it—*like me.* Her hair is dishwater gray and looks to be growing in from her last hospital-issued cut. When she is calm, her eyes have a look of emptiness to them, which could change at any moment if she grows agitated. Paul had told Lola that until a good mix of medication was found to keep her in a docile state, Edna was a classic case of Dr. Jekyll and Mr. Hyde.

A woman of few words, Edna's primary issues seem to be around anxiety. During the little time Lola has known the woman she'd asked Lola at least forty times "Is everything all right?" and "Are we going to die?" Lola knows she might tire of Edna's constant questions quickly.

To Lola's right sits her roommate, pink-haired Tina. Tina, Lola learned the night before after lights out, is a cutter. She's had several suicide attempts and has every intention of seeing her plan to fruition "as soon as they stop watching me." Lola worries about the young girl, who can't be a day over twenty and wishes she didn't feel obligated to take her on as another rescue project. *Maybe Rabbit could have a friend. I have to stay focused and try to convince them to let us out of here once and for all. I have to make this about me—whoever I am—and not everyone else in this nuthouse.*

Lola's thoughts are interrupted when Edna's head snaps up. Her suddenly hateful eyes lock onto Lola's as she mouths the words "Watch. Your. Back. Cunt."

Lola resists looking behind her to see who Edna could be talking to. She knows people aren't always what they first appear and wonders if Tina saw Edna's outburst too. Lola averts her eyes and chooses not to respond to the old woman, hoping her hostility will dissipate.

"Why are you here?" Justin asks Lola, entirely ignoring the old woman as though he's heard it a thousand times.

Lola could hug him.

"I'm not really sure," she replies. "They say I hear voices."

"You've been here a long time, you know. Tina said so. Didn't they tell you? Just 'cause you're new in this part of the joint doesn't mean you haven't been locked up forever. I'm here 'cause I hit stuff and break stuff and I like to pull fire alarms. It's a fun noise!"

Lola laughs, nodding as though she often spends spare Friday nights running around seeing how many alarms she can set off. *Don't give Clare any new ideas.*

"Hey! You! Pretty lady! Come sit with us!" Justin calls to a young nurse walking by.

She pivots to greet him.

"Hi Justin. How are you doing today? Staying out of trouble?" she asks. "Edna, Lola, Tina, how are you?" Justin smiles—displaying half-eaten ham sandwich chunks in his grin. "Yes, ma'am." He salutes the nurse, soggy sandwich in hand.

"We're good," Tina reports. "Edna's crabby as usual. Nothing new with me: Three days in and I want out already."

***

Frog

"I hate Jell-O. Can't trust anything that moves on its own. Don't believe everything Host says."

My name is Frog. I'm twenty. I don't know what else you want me to say. I have five sisters and one brother. I guess you would call them that. I live in Host's head. I don't mind it much. I'm not one to complain. I'm the fifth child. Host's doctors—halters—call me the fifth persona, alter or voice. I hate that shit. But that's what you get when Host has Multiple Personality Disorder (MPD). Oh, Maria told you that already. Figures. Either way, no one wants to understand that you actually do exist with MPD. It's worse when they call it DID. Screw that. Sometimes, I feel bad for Host. Her real name is Lola, but no one will tell you that. Maria says we can't get too attached. Other times, I'm angry at Host and am glad she doesn't get a name. Try being named after an amphibian. It's karma.

I don't like the way things are done here. I only came to help Tim. Now I can't leave. There was a fight and he wasn't winning. Tim thinks he's a better fighter than he is, but he's a good guy. He's just getting old and tired. My specialty is the martial arts. I can throw a round house higher than Host's head. Not bad when you're working in a chick body. Someone should give me a black belt for that. I wonder if Host will ever let me go.

After our first fight together, Tim showed me how to throw my first legit punch. He's the closest thing I'll ever have to a father. It's not my fault that I didn't know how to keep my thumb protected. That won't ever be an issue again. We made the girls learn too. We want them to know how to protect themselves, and Host, if they ever have to. It gets pretty sketchy living in a nuthouse, you know.

There's a halter named Paul who I like. When I do get to be in charge—which hardly ever happens around here with Maria in the way—I like to hang out with Paul. He's sort of like a security guard here. He's the one that restrains the crazies when they get out of control. There's another guy, Tom, who does it too, but he's not as cool as Paul. And he's new. I've wondered sometimes, if Paul has alters in him too. Host says if he did he'd be living in there with her, eating orange Jell-O every Friday like the rest of them.

So what else? Well, I like philosophy. Sometimes, when Host is asleep, I wake her up to read. I like reading about the different ways people see the world. I spend a lot of time thinking about how we alters got in here and why. I know we each came at a point in Host's life where she needed us most. That part, I get. But what I wonder about is if we really help her. By fighting her battles for her—literally in me and Tim's case—she's not getting the chance to stand up for herself. Here's an example of what I mean. When Maria came along, it was because Host was a freak. She looked like a boy after a bad case of head lice and no one wanted to be her friend in her new school. So Maria comes in and makes friends for Host. Now, Host has trouble making friends. I mean, I know she does okay with the crazies, but that's not the kind of friend I mean. I mean a normal halter friend – a person who isn't locked up.

Maybe I overthink things. I've done reading that the only way to "cure" Host is to have us all merge into one personality—hers—and have it be the dominant personality. I can tell you there is no way Tim and me are going for that. For starters, we're guys. Second? We aren't gay. And I can just see Clare and Zoe on a man hunt. Gross. I don't even want to think about it.

So if merging isn't an option, I'm with Tim. We need to get Host physically out of this place. Once we're out, we can figure out a way to help her survive without merging us at all. Think about it, between the eight of us, we have enough skills to patch a life together, even with Host in charge most of the time.

Let's see, what else? Oh! I know. One thing I really hate about being an alter is that the halters refer to us as being a disorder. That really pisses me off. I'm just as real as Host or any halter out there. It makes me feel like I'm invisible. Unimportant. Truth is all I want to do is write my name in the snow, if you know what I mean, and it sure as hell wouldn't be Lola or Frog that I wrote. Maybe Socrates or Augustine. Let's face it. I'll never get to change my name or even be me. I'm stuck in here. I hate it.

Have I talked enough? I really don't want to listen to Maria. She says I need to participate more. I think she should have been a teacher, or maybe president. She certainly thinks she is. Where's Rabbit? Isn't it her turn to talk?

***

October 15, 1994

Lola

Frog came on a day we all remember well. And they can laugh at me or scold me all day long for naming him Frog, but he really is one. He just hopped right in there to help out. And it didn't hurt that it was amphibian day at the loony bin. There was this guy, Mike, in the high security wing. Of course, I'm not judging him for that. Most of the time, I've been there too. But because it was the day of our visit from the Natural History Museum, the Rosewood staff was busy. They weren't paying much attention. Neither was Tim, apparently.

Either way, the patients had more freedoms than usual. Mike kept staring at me—all through some woman's explanations of how frogs breathe in water—and I knew something wasn't right. I tried not to look at him but every time I did, he made strange faces, usually involving his tongue. At first, I thought it was funny. Clare did too. Then, she dared me to stick my tongue out at him. That's when things got out of control quickly.

Mike had me up against a wall before I knew what was happening. I called for Tim, I really did. But he didn't answer. Mike's hands were squeezing my throat and it took a good two minutes before any of the orderlies even noticed. Thankfully, other patients noticed and began screaming and pointing—but before any of the orderlies could get to us, Frog had already arrived.

I'm not sure what was more jarring—the feeling of Frog entering my body that first time, or watching Mike land on his behind as my legs kicked at him on auto—Frog—pilot.

Frog has a philosophy that it was fate. That he would have come into me that day either way. But I don't agree. I think he was born out of necessity. Maria and Tim can't do everything all day every day. They have to have lives too. I can't imagine what it's like living in a part of someone's brain, or even foot, which is often the case for Tim when he's looking to escape.

Chapter Six:
Rabbit

A frazzled woman scurries into the room ten minutes late. She takes her seat next to Lola.

"Sorry I'm late, everyone. Rough start to the morning," she says.

Her frizzy blonde hair and multi-colored scarfs remind Lola of something her mother would have worn or picked up for under $5 at a second hand shop. Her soda pop bottle glasses make her eyes bulge out like a insect's.

God! How horrible can one person's eyesight be? Lola asks herself with a silent chuckle.

The therapist's long, burgundy colored dress is covered with a hand knitted multi-colored sweater that matches the scarf perfectly.

"Is everyone all set for check-in?"

Tina jumps right in.

"I'm doing fine. I wish they'd stop with the checking on us so much. My new roommate came alive yesterday. Did you notice, Ann? The first day or two she thought she was a rabbit or something," Tina says.

Ann, whom Lola assumes is the therapist for this wing, is not discreet about leering at Lola.

Lola slumps into her chair.

Turning back to Tina, as if Lola doesn't have a voice of her own, Ann asks the pink-haired girl what she means.

"Ask her yourself!" Tina says, clicking her chewing gum and crossing her arms over her chest. Chewing gum isn't usually allowed in groups and this bothers Lola, or maybe, Maria.

With an entire room of mostly-strangers staring at her and silence so awkward it propels her heart into a whole new rhythm, Lola finally speaks. *You better be proud of me, Maria.*

"Apparently I've been stuck inside myself for a while now. I've let my alters do my talking. But you probably already know this." Lola lets out a nervous giggle.

"Well hello! It's nice to have *you* with us today, Lola," Ann says.

"Thanks."

"Is there anything you'd like to check in with the group about?" Ann asks. "Are you settling in?"

"Well, this is really pretty new to me. I'm not sure where I have been and still feel pretty foggy. I'm used to my alters doing my talking for me. So maybe I can just listen for today," Lola says, trying to be polite.

"Okay then, who would like to check in next?" Ann asks.

"Are we gonna die?" Edna asks.

"No, Edna. We're okay. You're okay."

Lola is impressed with the patience Ann exhibits in reassuring the older woman. She can't imagine how many times the therapist has answered that question.

"I have a thing!" Justin announces, springing from his chair with both hands in the air. "That new girl in the druggie hall. She's cute. Why is she here and does she have a boyfriend?"

"What new girl?" a man in his late 40s asks.

"You know, the one with the big tits," another chimes in.

Justin laughs.

"Yeah. Her, dude."

"Well, what else is there?" Justin asks with a chuckle, slapping hands with his crony.

Tina groans.

"It's always all about tits with guys," Tina says, rolling her eyes. "I need to figure out a way to become a lesbian."

***

Rabbit

"I feel like I've fallen into a rabbit hole and there's no way out."

I'm Rabbit and I'm fourteen. I'm lonely as hell. My birthday was two weeks ago and no one even noticed. They wonder why I cut. How else will I get any attention? Yeah, there are lots of us in here. But no one my age. It sucks. I get sick of looking out for Sam. Sam gets spoiled. Zoe gives her anything she wants. It's why Host gets in trouble so much for having stuff in her room that she shouldn't. If Sam wants it, Zoe makes Host get it for her. Thank goodness Zoe and Host don't have real kids. We'd get kicked out of here and be living in the streets. Do they kick people out of nuthouses? Where would we go?

I may be fourteen but I'm the smartest one of us. I know how to do things the others can't. If I had a superpower it would be anything to do with technology. Whenever something's broken around here, I ask the staff to let me look at it before they send it out to fix it. It pisses me off because they think Host is a genius. Some sort of computer wizard. Ha! She wouldn't even know how to sign onto the Internet.

I wish Zoe would collect broken iPods instead of all the crap she calls treasures. We could make a fortune on those. Maybe if Host would focus, we could even find a way to escape. I want to know what it's like to hang out with real—normal—kids my age. I don't know why I was born and most of the time I wish I wasn't.

I can't say I never get Host in trouble myself. Those scars on her ankles? Those are from me. Sometimes, I cut and it's not just for me. It's also to hurt her. I don't know if it's that I want to feel pain, or if it's that I want *her* to feel pain; probably both. At least when I cut, the others pay attention. Yeah, they yell at me and stuff, but who cares. Tim and Maria aren't my parents—even though they think they are. The fact is that we are all orphans. If anyone is our parent, it's Host, and that's a scary thought. Most of the time, she just sits, staring out the window and letting us live our lives inside her. But is that really a life? And whose life? Don't ask Frog. He'd go on and on and on. Nobody wants to listen to his theories on *that*.

I heard there's a halter named Tina everyone thinks I should spend some time with. Yeah. Not. I've done enough listening to know that Tina's got problems of her own. I'm not really into the idea of "you have so much in common, you both cut and you both want to escape." It takes more than that in common to form a friendship. And that pink hair? Ridiculous. But maybe.

What else is ridiculous is my name. Can't say it's not something Frog and I haven't bonded over. It could be worse. Psycho Host could have called me Bunny. I'd have killed her, and myself in the process. If I was ever to become a halter, I'd find a way to change it. I'd want a name that people took seriously. Maybe Susan. Maybe Margo. I'm not sure. If I was a halter, I'd go to college and study to become a scientist. I want to do lab experiments and find solutions to problems. If I have anything in common with anyone, it's Tim.

They think I'm depressed because I don't talk a lot. The truth is, they don't ask. I actually have a lot to say but no one seems all that interested in my opinion because they think I'm a still a kid. I don't think age has anything to do with anything when you're an alter. Again, my opinion doesn't really count. Maybe, if I gave Tina a chance, she'd listen. Pink's not *that* bad. At least she's an independent thinker, unlike *some* people we know.

***

April 20, 2000

Lola

Rabbit arrived around Easter. Other residents were visiting with relatives. No one showed up for me. Maria had to take over for most of that day. But I did get to participate in the animals expo put on by the Natural History Museum. Of course, most of the animals they brought in were bunny rabbits, with it being Easter and all. I know Frog hates his name and Rabbit probably does too. But what choice did I have, really? A girl can only be so creative with so many alters. Maybe I should leave the naming up to the others from now on.

Either way, the day Rabbit was born was a lonely one for me. Maria doesn't like it when I spend time with my human family. She prefers I think of my alters as my only family. The therapists here say that's not healthy for me, but I don't trust them. Who would trust people who can't seem to make any progress in all these years? If therapists knew what they were doing, wouldn't I—we—be out by now? We are frustrated.

Holidays in a mental hospital stink. They do their best. I'll give them that. On Easter, it's ham and au gratin potatoes. We get the best rolls too. Christmas is turkey and gravy and mashed potatoes. There's something pretty lonely about not being allowed a tree in your room and having to share one with however many residents are on your floor at that time in the atrium. They can't understand why I dissociate. I can't understand why I wouldn't, living here all these years. Personally? I think it's the most sane way to go – to escape it with my mind seeing as I'm not allowed to leave of my own free will. Disassociating is like getting caught up in a good book. Other times, it's like taking a nap. Either I get to watch the alters live my life for me, or I get to tune it all out and just rest.

Mental hospitals get busy with intakes during the holidays. I never understood that, but they say it's because people can get lonely on the outside too. I don't remember being particularly lonely on the outside, just when my girlfriends started dating. But overall, I was pretty good at entertaining myself, even after Holly died. Maybe that's the benefit of having alters. I've pretty much always had Clare.

Easter of 2000 involved a huge egg hunt. Don't ask me how I can remember this. I remember the oddest of things and forget even stranger ones. But that year, the egg hunt was bigger than ever before. And, we were allowed to go outside. It's not often that this happens, so maybe that's why I remember it. A kid in his early twenties won the egg hunt. He was smiling from ear to ear as he cashed in his eggs for hospital privilege cards.

We get those here. They're supposed to work as incentives to keep us on our best behavior. The trouble is they can be taken away as quickly as they are given out so I've given up trying to earn them. Between Rabbit's cutting and Clare's dares, it's nearly impossible to hang on to those things. I know it disappoints Maria when I lose them, but it's easier not to care. Besides, what good is a phone call home if I'm not even sure anyone would answer? I think I'd forget about me too if I were them. It's been how many years?

Chapter Seven:
Samantha

Lola

"You're looking happy today, Lola," Dr. Hillcrest notes, peering over his wire-rimmed glasses. "Take a seat."

"Hi." Lola exhales as she sits on the couch across from his desk. "I'm glad to be here."

"I hear you are settling in to the new wing well," Dr. Hillcrest says. "Where would you like to start today?"

"Well, I spent some time journaling. I've gone through about twenty of Mom's letters. I decided the best way to approach this might be making a list of the questions and concerns I'm having," Lola says. "I feel like there's a lot to catch up on and I don't know how we're going to be able to get to it all in an hour."

"Well, there's really no rush. We will meet three times a week and you have group," Dr. Hillcrest says. "We need to go slowly with this, anyway."

"I understand that but I'm sure you can also understand my position, Dr. Hillcrest. I feel like I've lost a great chunk of my life and I'm anxious to figure this all out so I can go back to living," she says, unsure if she even means it but sure the alters do.

"Yes. I can appreciate that," he says. "Where would you like to start?"

"I think the first thing I'd like to do is see my exact diagnosis," Lola says, remembering what Tim asked her to do.

Lola takes her time looking at the diagnosis sheet Dr. Hillcrest hands her. She can't hear Tim mumbling in her frontal lobe because she refuses to.

ROSEWOOD HOSPITAL FOR MENTAL WELLNESS

Patient name: Lola A Murray

Doctor: Theodore M. Hillcrest, MD

Diag. Codes: X DSM-IV:

Axis I: 295.30 Schizophrenia, paranoid type

Axis II: Borderline Personality Disorder, Dissociative Identity Disorder

Axis III: V62.81 Relational Problem NOS,

Axis IV: institutionalized for several years since early adulthood

GAF: 38, above average intelligence

Problem(s) (treatment necessity): *Pt suffers from ongoing delusions & hallucinations. Pt becomes fixated for long periods of time while experiencing such hallucinations; staring blankly at* *walls or out windows. Pt believes she has at least six alters ranging in age from seven to 45. Experiences voices talking to her as well as one another. Client has engaged in moderate self-harm activities as a young adult and has a history of suicidal ideology. Client still exhibits characteristics of PTSD from witnessing the death of a friend at age 16. No current suicidal ideation. See treatment plan.*

Progress/Plan(s): *Client has experienced moments of lucidity since current medication change—the first time since hospitalization at age 22. Encouraging client to stay out and learn to manage alters. Hospitalized indefinitely until progress has been maintained for significant period.*

The words hit her hard. *Hospitalized indefinitely. They won't like this.* Seeing it all on paper makes it feel more real, but it isn't something Lola hadn't been prepared for.

She clears her throat before speaking. "Okay. Well, this is what I expected. That's good right? I mean, it's got to be a start. I'm curious about the suicidal stuff, though. I don't remember ever being suicidal…was that Rabbit? I don't feel suicidal now and I would think if a person was going to kill herself it might occur to her in my current situation," she says.

Dr. Hillcrest chuckles.

"Well, I'm glad to see your sense of humor shining through," he says. "When you first came to the state hospital you were put on suicide watch. You were so young. According to the notes from back then, you were engaging in self-harm activities like cutting and often talked about suicide."

Just like Tina, but that could have been Rabbit. Remember to ask Maria if Rabbit was around back then. Wait. I don't think she could have been. Too long ago. "But has any of that been going on since I've been working with you in the recent, say, decade?" Lola prompts.

"No, in the past two or so years that seems to have quieted."

"So if I'm not a danger to myself or other people, why do I have to be here?" Lola asks.

"It's not you that I'm worried about as much as the alters living inside of you, Lola. When you take on their emotions it changes you. I'm also worried that you simply cannot function when you go inside yourself. You sat for months on end unable to care for yourself. You stared out a window, physically, while whole other multiple lives lived inside your head."

Lola bows her head. "When can I see my mother?"

"She comes every other weekend. She comes on Sundays usually," Dr. Hillcrest says. "I'm not sure if she was here last weekend or not but it's possible you will see her this Sunday unless you'd like to have me call her to come earlier for a special visit?"

"Have you talked to her?"

"I did call her to let her know you were with us—lucid—again but I advised her to give me a week or so to work with you and told her not to get her hopes up. Families can be a lot of pressure for patients when they are just coming out of a dissociative state," Dr. Hillcrest said.

"Okay."

Dr. Hillcrest answers most of Lola's questions during the rest of the session. She is surprised to learn that five percent of people with her diagnosis kill themselves during its onset and wonders what helped her to get through that time period.

"What I'm wondering, Lola, is would you let me in?" Dr. Hillcrest is fixated on his client now. His eyes bore through her as if he wants to jump into her body to check out the alters' rooms in her brain.

"What do you mean?"

"I've done some research on hypnosis. I'm thinking that if we could do some work with each of the alters, it might help." Dr. Hillcrest's voice drifts. "The last time we tapped into your subconscious, it caused another alter to come out. I think that one was Sam, Samantha. I'd have to check my notes. But the youngest. We've done a lot of research since then. It's a risk but…"

"Yes! Let's do it." Lola beams. *Clare will* love *this.*

"Okay, I—we can start that another day. I want you to have some time to process all this. I've thrown a lot at you and there will be more. I do have some ideas of things you might also want to consider. These are techniques that have helped others who suffer from identity disorders and may work for you."

"Sure. I'll try anything."

"Well, there's journaling. I know you keep a journal from time to time, but I'm thinking it might be nice if you had your alters write in it. Have them leave messages for one another. Sometimes, it helps get them talking."

They talk to one another every day. They live together, for God's sake! They don't need to be writing love letters. "Okay," Lola says, unwilling to give away her secret. "I can get them to try that."

"Good. Good. And another idea is a video journal. I can see about getting you a video camera. But you will get to see them with me under hypnosis so that might not be needed. The key is to get you all talking so we can try to initiate a merge. When all the alters come together, that's about as close as we can call a cure," Dr. Hillcrest says. "I must warn you, though. There is no real cure. You will need to stay on meds even after you and the alters have merged."

"I understand," Lola says. This time, she's not lying or faking anything.

"It's going to be important that you make them feel safe. They need to learn to trust you the way you trust them. Let them know they are all aspects and fragments of you and that whoever or whatever hurt them is not someone or something you will allow to hurt them again. Even talk to them externally if you need to. Get to know every aspect of them. What they fear, what they hope and dream. This is a way of getting to know yourself and knowing yourself is key," Dr. Hillcrest says.

Lola's beginning to fade, wishing Maria was in the lobby—frontal lobe—to take over. But only Tim remains, silent, watching, listening. *This is too much.* "Okay."

"...and one of the most important things you can do is to try to get in touch with the children. Samantha, Rabbit, even Frog. You can do this with an exercise called left to right hand writing. You use your opposite of dominant hand, so, for you, it would be right, and have the children write down things like their names, ages, and feelings. Have them draw pictures. You will clearly be able to better understand them if you do this daily."

Yeah. I can see Frog wanting to sit down at a desk and write his name and age and draw me a picture with the wrong hand. Rabbit will bite my face off if I even ask. Maybe Samantha will do it if I can get Zoe to tell her to. This is ridiculous. "That sounds neat. I think they will like that," Lola says. "I'll ask, thank you, Doctor."

***

Samantha

"It's kinda smushy in here."

Hi! I'm Sam. I'm seven. Rabbit calls me the "new kid." But I'm not that new. I'm Zoe's favorite and that makes Rabbit mad. Whatever. I don't care what Rabbit thinks. Nobody does. She's a grump. Like Oscar the Grouch. Or Eeyore. Not like Peter Pan.

Today, Zoe is getting me plastic forks from the cafeteria. We're going to build a castle with them. Host says it's okay as long as we can make the castle pink. I don't really like pink but that's okay. If I could make the castle any color, it would be blue. Blue like the sky. The sky looks tasty, like blueberry cotton candy. Zoe tries to make everything pink. Whatever.

The day I was born was the day Host got hypnotized. That's when they put you in a trance and stuff comes out. Zoe says I came out because I'm the best part of Host. But I think Zoe is the best part of Host. She's nice to me. They all are, mostly, except Rabbit. But that's just because she's jealous. I don't want any more kids to come here. I like being the youngest. But Zoe wants more. She likes collecting things. She says more are coming. She says Host moves slow. Zoe says most girls like Host have more than two dozen kids. I'm glad Host moves slow. I want things to stay the way they are forever. Do you wanna play a game with me? My favorite is Connect Four. I also love Battleship. Tim taught me that game the day I was born. Now, he plays it with me when he wants me to be quiet. I don't mind. I like spending time with Tim and I like that game even more. I win every time no matter what, unless I play with Rabbit.

**

May 22, 2007

Lola

Sam was probably the most expected of the alters. When you live in a mental hospital this long, one thing you are used to hearing about is a person's "inner child." "Love yourself like you are you own best friend." "Nurture your inner child." These are the kind of things they say to us—constantly—to help us to be nicer to ourselves. Of course, because of Rabbit, they see me as a cutter, a self-mutilator. So I probably hear this more than, say, the narcissistic patients. It sort of makes me laugh. I'm anything *but* a self-mutilator. I'm not sure why they don't get that it's her doing it, not me. I've told them a hundred times. They just stare at me like I'm crazy.

Anyway, it was May. People were excited about Memorial Day coming. I had nowhere to go. I didn't have privilege cards and high max patients can't leave hospital grounds anyway. Others were preparing for a three-day reprieve weekend with friends and family and our group was doing a section on loving our inner child. I remember sitting in group therapy all week thinking, "is Rabbit my inner child?" But I knew that couldn't be right. Rabbit's too independent. Even at eight, Rabbit was more of an adult than she ever was a child. Besides, she was so quiet back then we rarely heard from her.

So, in came Sam, during hypnosis. Like her big sister Zoe. And what a delight she was. From the moment she entered me, she brought everyone joy—even the boys. Maria and Zoe mothered her and Frog and Tim babysat her. I'm not sure Clare and Rabbit noticed, but that's okay. They have their own lives too.

Sam's a Gemini. Zoe swears this is why she gets along with all of us. She can turn from a happy, sweet little girl in love with Peter Pan to a mini-Tim in minutes. She hardly ever complains or cries. She does what she's told and is able to entertain herself. Really, she's every mother's dream. I think Zoe hopes to one day get out and take her with her. But Zoe's like that, always collecting things.

Inner children are supposed to teach us things about ourselves. The problem is, Sam's not my inner child. Sam's a child who lives in me. They don't seem to understand the difference. To them, Sam's just another of my imaginary friends. Or, a split off my personality. I can tell you, that's not the case. There is no part of my personality interested in Peter Pan or mechanics. Nope. Sam's a person all her own and no one could convince me—or her—otherwise.

Chapter Eight:
Host

"Dragonfly!"

An animated Stella bounces—*not bad for a 70-year-old*—up to Lola before she's ready for it. Before Lola can catch her breath, Stella's arms are around her shoulders, pulling her into a snug embrace.

Her mother smells of familiar coconuts and peppermint. It's a smell Lola adored as a child. Now she isn't quite so sure.

Lola feels like a child who's just discovered they'd been given up for adoption and is meeting their birth mother for the first time. *I still need to find out why Maria didn't tell me Mom's been visiting all these years.*

She tolerates her mother's hug for much longer than she wants to. When it finally ends, she suggests they move to the far end of the visiting lounge in the atrium. She can feel all eyes on her as she settles in.

Stella looks the same as she had in Lola's mind and Lola wonders if that is because she's been visiting her all these years. *Do Maria's memories get trapped in my head too? How is that possible?* She isn't sure, but is relieved for the familiarity either way.

Stella's frizzy gray hair is tied into a tight bun on the top of her head. She wears a soft lavender shirt that accents her curvy figure. Her hands give away her years and worries with their deep lines.

Face this. She holds answers. She cares. No more running, Lola tells herself.

"...and you're very brave, Lola. You were tired. You were scared. You wanted it to be quiet," Stella says. "I can't believe you're finally here in the world with us again! How *are* you? How have you been? I've missed you something awful! That Maria is a very nice...er...person. But it's you I've missed."

Lola finally sits on the plush sofa in the Rosewood visitor's lounge and motions for her mother to do the same. Stella sits across from her on the edge of a twin couch. She looks like a child at Christmas, barely able to contain herself.

God, I wish she would stop staring at me. Too. Much. Pressure. What does she want from me? Does she not get how mortifying this is?

"I'm good, Mom. A little confused. And I want out of here. How have you been?" Lola asks.

"Oh they can't make you stay long now, Lola. Dr. Hillcrest said only a couple of weeks. They were just waiting for you to come back and be done with those silly voices. He said you've been back for over a week now!" Stella beams. "I tried telling them you've had these imaginary friends all your life and they weren't going to hurt anyone."

They are not imaginary! "I have a lot of questions," Lola begins, praying her mother will be receptive and not give her the vague sorts of answers she once did so many years ago.

"Lay them on me, Lola. I'll answer anything you need," Stella says.

Lola exhales.

"Dr. Hillcrest gave me the letters you've been writing all these years. Thank you, by the way."

Stella nods. "Oh, Lola! Of course! You're my girl! That hasn't changed!"

"Why did my father leave us?"

"Oh, Lola. Are you sure you want to know that?"

"Mom, I need to know everything," Lola says, not breaking eye contact.

"Okay. Well, I guess the best way to answer that is that he wasn't really ours in the first place," Stella says. "Your father was actually my boss. I was young and naïve. He was married to another woman and when he found out I was pregnant he wanted me to have an abortion. Of course,

I could never do th—anyway, he was never in the picture, Lola. I'm sorry."

Lola takes a moment to process her mother's words. She can't deny the sting of learning she is the product of an affair. *How did I not know this all my life? Why didn't I ask her when I was a teenager or something? This is exactly what Maria hates about me. I never ask enough questions and don't want to face reality.*

"But there was a letter. You said my father tried contacting you years later and asked about me?"

"Yes. His wife died about ten years ago. He came to 'claim' me as though you and I had been just pining for him all those years. Ha! Asshole," Stella says. "Can you imagine, Lola? By then I had Travis for *years* and was perfectly happy. The only thing missing was you. It's so good to have you back, Sweetheart."

***

"I'm not so sure I want to be back or am even strong enough to be back."

My name is Lola but my voices—alters—call me Host. I really don't care what they call me. It used to bother me. Host is such a boy-sounding name. On second thought, sometimes it bothers me.

I can't decide. I have trouble deciding anything. It's not easy to have so many opinions floating around your head. And don't get me started on the opinions of the people who are supposed to be helping me get better. They haven't seemed to help anything for three decades now, so who needs them? Clare says opinions are like bad days: Everybody has them, but they're best to ignore and try to forget about. Unless, of course, the opinion is hers. Clare makes me laugh. She makes everyone laugh.

In a way, we've already met. I'm the one who's been telling you about each of my alters' birthdays and how they came about living inside of me. I let the others' speak first, because that's our pattern. They speak, then me. As for me, it's hard to know exactly who I am when I've never been allowed to live my own life. I've been living in the Rosewood Hospital for Mental Wellness since my twenties. I'm fifty or fifty-one now. I can't remember and don't really care. Maria would know. Ask her. I'm not so sure it—this place—it makes me well, but my medications are free and I really don't know any other way. The last time I didn't take my meds I landed in here. At least here I'm sure I get what I need. Every day I take the same thing—Abilify 15 mg, 1 tab po q day, Fluoxetine Hydrochloride 20 mg, 1 tab po q day, and Klonopin 1 mg, 1 tab po qhs and ½ tab po prn, Risperdal 4 mg, 1 tab bid. No grapefruit. Avoid alcohol. Avoid excessive sun.

I don't really understand what any of that means, I'm just reading it to you, but Maria does. Maria takes care of me. She's my oldest alter. But Clare's my favorite. She's the most fun. She makes me laugh. She makes everyone laugh. Sorry, I already told you most of this. Sometimes, I get forgetful, then remember. It's probably my medications. Or, it's having people jump in and out of my brain all day that keeps me distracted. It's why it's impossible for me to make and keep friends. Clare helps me get friends. Making friends has never been easy for me. In my whole life, I've only had a few. I don't like to talk about that. And the friends here, I just end up trying to help them. Then they leave or go away. Even worse, they don't get along with my alters and that's the end of that.

I don't remember much since high school. But I can tell you about growing up. My mom, Stella, raised me pretty much by herself. I never knew my father. I can't even call him dad because a dad would have been around. Tim—my oldest boy alter—is the closest thing to a father I have ever had. But we don't talk much. I have a stepfather who is nice enough. But I don't really know him well. I've been in here so long I've begun losing my connections to the outside world. The alters say this is a big problem. In some ways, I agree. In others, I don't see what's wrong with staying at Rosewood forever. I mean, the people here are family to me and the staff makes sure I am taken care of.

I think about what it would be like to leave here. The alters—all but Samantha—want out. I have days where I just want to scream to Tim to get us out of here and let him take over my mind for good. It might be nice to be an alter rather than a host. I don't think they understand how much pressure it can be to be the leader. I'm not a natural leader and never was.

In first grade, I was picked to be the line leader. It was the first or second day of school. I had no hair because my mother had shaved my head bald after a bad case of head lice. My mother is practical, or was...most of the time, anyway. She figured it would be best to just start over and didn't put much thought into what it would be like for me to start school looking like a freak. Did me or Maria tell you this already? I wish Clare had been around back then. She would have helped me. She would have made my bald head cool. Or even Zoe, she would have told me to tell them all I had cancer so they would have to be nice to me. But it was Maria who showed up. I don't think Maria likes my real mother much. And it's probably because of the bald head thing. She doesn't tend to talk about her a lot. Maria likes to think of herself as my real mother instead. Sometimes, I feel like she's right.

I don't remember anything before first grade. And the rest of school was pretty hard for me too. I had a few close friends. My best friend was Holly. I can't talk about her because it hurts too much. She died when I was sixteen. It was my fault. They say it wasn't, but I know the truth. I should have never asked her to get me out of the house that day. I was mad at my mother. She wouldn't let me get my license.

The only good thing about losing Holly was waking up in the hospital and meeting Clare. Clare became my new best friend but it will never be the same. There's a difference between being friends with a voice—alter—in your head and a real-life person. And that's the thing about being here at Rosewood. Nowhere else in the world would anyone understand. They get the differences between the voices and the people we see in the "real world." And when you're lucky, you make a friend who also understands just how real your alters are. Those are the kind of friends you like to keep around. Sadly, it never lasts for long. One of you gets discharged, released, or transferred. Sometimes, we even lose friendships to medication.

I'm sick of losing people. It's part of why I'm helping Tim and the alters get us out of here. I want to be able to figure out who I am and create my own life. But I'm not sure I'm going to be successful. For most of my life I've used my alters to help me survive. Some days, I hate them. But most days? They are my best friends. They are also my worst enemies.

People say the only way to cure what I have is to bring all the alters together and merge them into one personality. That personality would be mine. That is so hard for me to understand. I'm already me and they are already them. Why would we bother to merge? That would be like taking a football team of players—each with his own talents—and saying "okay let's put you all into one player." What would the point be? For starters, you wouldn't have enough people to play on the team. But you also would never be able to build the perfect athlete. I guess they aren't trying to build a team or anything close to perfect. What they want is to build me. I'm not sure how I feel about that. I'm already built, aren't I?

Chapter Nine:
Crosstalk

The hospital cafeteria has its usual smell of Windex and burnt toast that evening. Lola inhales as she approaches her now regular dining companions and fellow patients in the minimum security wing.

"Hey all," she says, plopping onto a plastic stool attached to the long dining table. She looks at the main course, tuna melt, and pulls it to her lips. She scrunches her nose at how bland it tastes. She reaches for the salt and pepper shakers and begins to work them both over her plate to get at least some sort of flavor on the bland hospital fries.

"Hey there!" Justin smiles, his almond eyes staring at the tangerine on Lola's tray. "You gonna eat that?"

"All yours," Lola says, grateful that someone in this place knows her well enough to know she doesn't eat fruit.

"Are we gonna die?" Edna asks.

"No, Edna. We're fine. Eat your supper," Lola pushes. *Is that how I sound when I'm out of it?*

The old woman glares at Lola, who wants to laugh as Edna's top teeth become

104

loose and distract her. She fumbles to get them to stick back to the roof of her mouth.

"What did you and your mom talk about?" Tina asks.

"Basically about everything that has been going on all these years. How she missed me. How it isn't my fault. How she can't wait to have me back home," Lola says.

"Are you being released?" Tina asks.

"I'm working on it," Lola says between bites of her sandwich. "I don't trust anyone around here. But if I have a say in it I'm getting the hell out of this place. I just have to keep my voices quiet and stop getting in trouble."

"I hear ya about trust," Tina says. "I don't really care if I stay here. Doesn't matter where I die. But they never leave me alone. Would be so much easier on the outside."

"Easier to die?" Lola asks.

"Yep," Tina says, snapping her gum. "Food here sucks."

"I lovvvvvvve the food! You don't want that? Can I have it?" Justin asks.

"Yup." Tina pushes her tray toward Justin, saving the tangerine for herself. She picks at it while Edna readjusts her teeth and plays with a fry.

"Can I ask you something?" Lola turns to face Tina.

"Sure. What's up?"

"Why do you want to die?"

Tina laughs. "Why would I want to live?"

"I'm serious," Lola says, wondering if it will help her better understand Rabbit. "You're young and smart and pretty. You have the whole world in front of you. A whole lifetime. You haven't been here that long. You can still have any life you want."

"That's the thing. That's what people see. But that's not the truth," Tina says. "My life was over when I was nine and my mother decided I wasn't worth sticking around for. Since then? All downhill."

"But don't you have other people— family—who love you and care about you?" Lola asks.

"Not everyone's like you, Lola. Most people don't stick around to see how the nutcase turns out," Tina says. "I want to die. Leave it alone."

"Am I okay?"

"Yes! Edna! You're okay," the group says in unison.

As Lola listens to her Rosewood friends talk over the rest of their meal, she begins to think about what they have in common:

106

Their voices. People keep on going – hoping someone will hear them. If they are heard, they can finally come alive again.

Tina is manic by the time they return to their room for a two-hour block of after dinner free time. She paces the tiny space and rambles on about plans to get out of Rosewood "one way or the other." Lola sighs, sits on her bed, and tries to ignore her frantic roommate. *She sounds just like the alters. They are going to be angry. They want to have a meeting tonight. I can't concentrate with this girl in here.*

She watches from her bed as Tina fools around with her iPod and whines about being bored with her music. The girl, who can't weigh over 100 pounds, brushes her hair twice, makes her bed three times, and straightens her personal items on her nightstand at least four in a matter of ten minutes. Lola wishes she would just leave.

"Bored?" she asks, hoping Tina will get the hint.

"What else? This place blows," Tina says.

"I heard Mary has some new books and magazines down in the library. Maybe that would help?" Lola suggests.

Tina shakes her head. "Been there, done that. I think it's the new meds. Every time

I get used to my meds they adjust them. I'm so sick of this," she says.

Lola can relate, but is glad for the latest tweak of her own drug cocktail.

"Has your doctor talked about when you can get out of here?" Lola asks.

"Nah. I'm still a risk to myself. Damn straight I am!" Tina says, holding out her arms so Lola can get a good view of the angry red scars on her wrists. Some are fresh. Others are just white lumps that look like stretch marks now. "What I don't get is why they even care. It's *my* shit life. I should have a choice to end it if I want to."

"I don't think they're big on free will," Lola laughs.

"No, they sure aren't. I hate them!" she says. "Have you seen my lipgloss? There's a new hottie upstairs. I think he's in for heroin and crack. At least he'll be entertaining."

"It's on the bathroom sink," Lola says, aware of her emerging role as Tina's surrogate mother.

"Great! Thanks!" Tina says, leaping off her bed to get dolled up.

When Tina finally leaves with more makeup than even Clare would approve of, Lola finally breaks down. She cries for the twenty-two-year-old Lola. She cries for the alters. She hurts for her mother and family and time she's missed. *They're right,* Lola tells herself. *We need to get out of here. We need to start our lives. Maria? Where are you?*

***

"Host! Cut it out. We only have a limited window! Save your tears for another time," Tim begs. "Join us, please. I'm calling order to this meeting. Today's purpose is to figure out how to get out of here once and for all. Host? Are you *ever* going to join us?"

Lola isn't listening. She continues to cry into her hospital-issued pillow.

"It's no use, and you know it. Leave her alone and let's just get this done without her. I'll fill her in after it's done," Maria, flush-faced, says. "It's not like she usually comes to meetings anyway. Let her be."

"And I can take the minutes," says Rabbit. "We can read them to her later."

Tim glares at the pair but softens when Rabbit returns his glare with a smile. Rabbit rarely smiles.

Clare yawns. "How long is this gonna take? Ya'll don't seem to remember that I've got a show to prep for."

"Do you want to write stand up for a bunch of loonies for the rest of your life?

You'll never have a chance to get to the big stage if you don't work with us. It's *your* fault she got in trouble last week. We all need to work on the same *team* or we'll be in here *forever*," Zoe says.

Clare clicks her gum. "Whatever. It was *hilarious* and you know it, Zoe. Just hurry please, ya'll. We never get anywhere with this crap. It's like wheel-spinning or whatever."

Maria motions to Tim to continue while Frog and Sam argue over a game of hangman.

"Okay, so here's how I see it. That halter—Dr. Hillcrest—wants her to go under hypnosis. This is our chance. If we can find a way to get her to say there are no more alters—that she's cured—we can get her out of here the easy way," Tim says. "I mean, I've got this place figured out as far as escaping the hard way. But it would be so much easier with a discharge. I can't see Host being able to survive without some sort of transition plan. Gotta agree with the doc on that."

"Well, obviously we don't want to do it the hard way. Imagine what could happen if she gets caught trying to sneak out or something. Remember what happened last time? Host doesn't have the physical strength to pull another stunt like that. She was younger then. It wasn't your brightest idea, Tim," Maria says.

"It was better than any idea you've had," he retorts.

"Great plan! Meeting adjourned then, ya'll?"

"Oh, be *serious*, Clare! Your stupid comedy crap can wait," Zoe says.

"Yes, ma'am," Clare says, saluting Zoe. "Whatever you say, ma'am."

"How old *are* you? Act your age or something *please*," Zoe says. "Sam acts older than you!"

"Age doesn't…" Maria cuts Rabbit off.

"Enough, you three. We can't get anything done with your bickering. If you don't want to be here, Clare, leave," Maria says. "Zoe, Rabbit, please try to focus! This is important! I thought you two wanted out?"

"Well, finally. Someone with some sense. I think I will. Thank you muchly, mother Maria. Toodles, ya'll." Clare blows the group a kiss, leaving a red smudge on her right hand as she bows and exits the meeting.

"Thank *gawdddd*!" Zoe sighs.

Samantha giggles and Frog begins a game of solitaire, shrugging.

"Wanna play Uno with me?" Samantha asks Frog.

"Naw. What about War?" he says.

"Okay, sure," Samantha says. "You deal."

"Guys! We can't get anything done with all the side talk! Everyone needs to pay attention so we can figure out a plan before Host comes back," Tim says. His voice is stern and deeper than usual. "Plenty of time for games later, Frog."

When the alters quiet, Tim starts where he left off, explaining that it's probably a good thing Host "can't be bothered" to attend today's meeting. "So my thinking, and I've talked to Rabbit about this, is that we need to all work together to make the halters believe we've merged. That may even mean making Host think it too. That's not going to be easy, especially with Clare around. We're going to need to find a way to shut her up."

Zoe snorts. "Yeah, good *luck* with that."

"Maybe we could like, bribe her?" Frog offers, cracking his knuckles.

"Or duct tape her mouth shut?" Rabbit suggests.

"That's useless. You know Host can hear us, even when we aren't speaking. We need to find a way to get Clare to sleep and it might be for a long time. Like a month or something so that we can get the halters to really believe Host is cured," Maria says. "How are we going to do that, Tim?"

"I don't think it's even possible. You bring up a good point. Host will know. So there's just no way we can do this without Host's help. Get her in here, Maria. She listens to you."

"All right, give me a few. I'll be right back. Hopefully, with Host. Be *nice* everyone. This isn't easy for her either. And it doesn't help with everyone giving her crap all the time."

Rabbit rolls her eyes. No one notices.

Maria returns thirty minutes later.

"She isn't interested in attending a meeting tonight, but she will talk to me. I need you all to make yourselves scarce so I can get, and keep, her full attention. She's all over the place tonight. Do you think you can all stay occupied and not butt in?"

"Unreal. You women drive me insane," Tim says. "Fine. Get it done. We'll reconvene later and figure out where to go after you get her on board."

The alters retreat to their respective living, not sleeping, areas. For Rabbit, this is Host's occipital lobe of the brain, for Sam, Host's belly button area. For Frog it's the left leg, Tim the right. For Zoe it's

113

the heart. Maria floats to Host's frontal lobe; where's she's most likely to be able to keep Host's attention.

"I'm not talking to you until you explain to me why you didn't tell me my mother's been visiting all these years," Lola tells her oldest alter.

Maria takes a moment to answer. "I was trying to protect you," she says softly.

"From what?"

"From everything."

"I don't even understand what that means," Lola says.

"I know you don't. I just need you to trust me. Do you trust me, Host?"

"This is just so hard. Everything. It's all so hard."

"I know this is hard. And trust is always hard. Heck, I still remember the days where you thought Tim and I were trying to kill you. You know that's not true now. We want what's best for you. I've only done what's best for you. I promise, I'll give you answers to everything soon. But first we need to work together to get out. We have a unique chance right now and can't afford to waste time," Maria says. "Don't worry about Tim. He's a man. He doesn't understand emotion like we do."

"I just don't get how he can demand I do this and try to make me do it now. He thinks it's easy being a host. Trust me, it's not. I can't even live my own life without everyone telling me what to do and how to do it," Lola says.

"I'm sure it is," Maria placates.

"You have no idea what it's like to try to do something and have seven voices screaming at the same time to do it a different way. I didn't choose this. I want out of here too. It's not like I want to be locked up in here, but the idea of leaving scares me."

"If it helps, I'm scared too," Maria admits. "I have no idea what it will be like for us all to leave. We haven't known anything else for thirty years. Heck, half of them don't even know what it's like outside these walls. Trust me, I'm petrified too."

"Exactly! Take Rabbit, for example. She thinks she's depressed now? She's just like Tina. Tina's probably better off in here, which is why she keeps coming back. Imagine what Rabbit would do if she had real knives to cut me with? And what about Sam? Sam won't know what to do with herself. To her, Disneyland is the hospital game room," Lola says. "They think it's so easy. It's not. They aren't the ones who have to trick everyone that they're cured. They aren't the ones who

115

will have to figure out how we eat. It's a lot of responsibility and Tim doesn't seem to get that."

Maria nods, and then remembers that Host can't see her. "I agree. I'm not sure he's thought much about what would happen from that perspective if we got out. That's something I'll bring up when I talk to him."

"Thank you for getting me, Maria. I promise I'm going to do my best. I get what they want me to do. They want me to fake that I've merged you all into me and that I'm cured. To make it seem like the meds are working. Tim forgets that I can hear his thoughts if I try hard enough. He's an idiot about that sometimes," Lola says. "I just need him to understand that I'm working on it. These people, staff and doctors, aren't stupid, you know. This is what they do. I'm not the first host they have come across and I certainly won't be the last. I'm just worried they'll be onto me."

"I completely understand. You never need to thank me. But I think Tim has a point. Between the new med change, the fact that you've stayed dominant personality for a full week now, and the hypnosis, the timing might be right for them to actually buy it. I think this might be a now or never type thing, Host. I'll help you however I can and I'll do my best to get Tim to lay off."

"Okay. I'm meeting with Dr. Hillcrest several times a week now, so I'll go as fast as I can. I need you guys to come up with a plan—a reasonable one—for how we're supposed to survive if I do get out of here, though. I can't think of everything."

"On it. I'll get Zoe on it too," Maria says. "I need you to reason with Clare, though. She can't be jumping in you and ruining it; even if it means giving up the comedy routine. See if you can get her to do it for us, instead of the halters, or something. She only listens to you. If even that."

"I'll figure that out. I'm thinking it may be okay for Clare to be Clare if they think we've merged. They will just see me as Lola, the improved, funnier version. Right?"

"I'm not so sure about that. Clare's a little too outrageous," Maria says.

"I'll think of something."

"Okay, goodnight. Try to get some sleep. I'll do my best to keep them quiet so you can rest. You have a lot ahead of you. I think one of the best things you can do is think about figuring out who you are, merged or not. It will be the best thing for you and the best thing for convincing the halters you're safe and okay to be set free," Maria says. "And Host? I'm proud of you."

"Thanks, Maria. Night," Lola sighs.

***

Maria

"Goodnight, Host, sleep well," I respond, hoping she does, but doubting it.

I really am proud of her. I try to lie to her minimally. And I will start thinking of a plan. The good thing about being an alter is you can delegate, so a big part of that will be Tim's territory. Rabbit's too. She's great for thinking things out. I have other things to deal with right now.

No one understands what it's like being the oldest alter. Tim says I whine a lot. But I'd like to see him in my position. There are some things even Tim doesn't know. To really understand my position, there's a lot you need to understand. For starters, as shiny and nice as Host's mom may appear, she wasn't the perfect mother. I do my best not to comment about her—Stella—when Host is listening but I'm not a perfect alter either. There are times when I just can't hold my tongue. Most times, though, I try to only speak well of the woman who gave birth to Host.

As far as I'm concerned, I'm Host's real mother. Being a mother comes with its share of ups and downs. There is the joy of seeing your child thrive and experience new things. In my case, with Host, there isn't a lot of thriving. But I can tell you, she has come a long way. The fact that she's lucid and remembering things; that she's participating in her own life and even in some of our meetings...those are all huge milestones for her.

I've been with Host for it all. I do what I can to protect her, even if she doesn't understand why. I'm always looking out for her best interest. Sometimes, I have to do things I'd rather not mention. One of those, though, is keeping secrets from Host and the other alters.

For years, Host's halter mother has been writing letters. Host has no clue. They were locked up in the doctor's office because he, like me, has been worried that she can't handle learning more about her past. But even more important, her mother has visited. Those are the days I rush to Host's frontal lobe and take charge. I never let Host visit alone. I know her mother has good intentions. I can't take that away from her. But she's pushy and likes to live in the past. I can't see where talking about Holly's death and Host's role in it would ever be helpful. I've seen Host go catatonic for months over a change in schedule. Do you really think she could handle the kind of information that sent her to the crazy house in the first place?

If you're judging me, and I expect that you are, think about this: Where was Host's mother all these years? Weekend visits don't cut it. I've been here, a part of everything, helping her through it all. I'm not the wicked witch you may want to believe. We all need a go-to person and cheerleader. I'm Host's. I just wish I had one of my own.

Sometimes I do feel guilty. There's this whole part of Host's life that she doesn't know about. I worry that she'll be angry with me when she finds out that I've kept all of this from her. But a mother's job is not to be her child's friend. It's to protect her. Sure, Host is over fifty years old, but she's still very much a child.

Tim and I don't agree on everything. But one thing we do agree on is that we need to get out of here. The thought of another decade in this place makes me sick. Host probably doesn't even remember this about herself, but she loves the ocean. My number one goal is to get her there again. The last time we went was when she was nine.

She can't afford another slip up. Reading those letters would set her back years. And the halter doctor doesn't understand that if we merge, we can't protect her. I wouldn't be afraid of merging if it wasn't for that. I'd do anything to give Host a shot at a real life. Her own life. But she's been locked up and sheltered too long to survive on her own. And that's partly my fault. It's something I'll have to rectify later, once we're finally out. In the meantime, I'm going to have to do my best to protect her and the other alters through the changes ahead. It's what a mother does.

Chapter Ten:
Finding Lola

Figure out who you are. Who are you, Lola? Lola spends the entire morning and afternoon the next day trying to answer this question. She knows Maria has a point. Being able to define herself to Dr. Hillcrest will go a long way in making him believe the alters have merged and that she is finally on the road to recovery. *Who are you, Lola?* No answers come. *Okay, then who do you want to be?*

She doesn't end her quest to find out who she wants to be at dinner that evening. In fact, she makes it a personal mission to watch people more closely to spot traits she does and doesn't like. *Worst case, I can reinvent myself.* While it feels ridiculous to try and reinvent herself at age fifty-one, she decides, what other choice does she have? *Those damn alters. Always bossing me around and telling me what to do. I'll never be able to do anything if they don't give me some time and space to figure it out. First of all, I'm* Lola, *not Host!*

"Can I have your yogurt?" Justin asks before Lola even has a chance to set down her tray.

A mooch. Not good. You don't want to be that. "Sure," she says, pushing her tray across the table to him.

"Thanks! You're the best, Lola," he says.

Appreciative. A good thing.

"Are we okay?" Edna asks.

The usual group chimes in, rolling their eyes, "Yes, Edna, we're okay."

The timeworn woman stares off at the cafeteria ceiling, making no attempt to eat. Her lips are pressed in a tight line and she rocks forward and backward just slightly on her plastic seat.

Old. Alone. Anxiety ridden. And in here. Not good. And no, we are most definitely not *okay! Add* clueless *to the list.*

"You can have all my food," Tina says, pushing her tray toward Justin too. "I'm on a hunger strike until they let us have unlimited and unmonitored Internet access, 'cause this is bullshit. I can't get in more than few YouTube videos and I sure as hell can't Skype! They wonder why I'm suicidal! Give me a break!"

Determined. Stubborn. Unrealistic. Not sure how I feel about most of those. But determined is good.

"Thanks!" Justin smiles at Tina, unconcerned that this is the third meal in a row his friend is skipping. He opens her milk carton as she rants on reasons and ways staff at Rosewood are unreasonable.

"…seriously, who do they think we are? They take every decision away from us and treat us like animals. We'd have more rights in a prison!" Tina says.

"I don't think inmates get any Internet," Lola says, wishing she hadn't.

"Oh. My. Gawwwwwd. For reals? Why don't you get a little nose to go with all that brown, Lola? I'm getting sick of you and how you kiss ass. You're just as crazy as we are—probably more! At least we know who we are!" Trish pronounces. "Are you even Lola today? Or are you Clare? You can't be Clare. She's fun."

"You're right. Sorry," Lola says, pushing her own tray toward Justin. "You can have mine too."

A new patient, Lindsay, sits down with the group before Lola has a chance to figure out what to do about Tina.

Lindsay is about five feet tall and Lola knows she weighs 136 pounds from overhearing her intake earlier in the nurses' station. This is Lindsay's fourth trip to Rosewood and she doesn't seem to mind being hospitalized. Her biggest complaint is that being hospitalized means she can't shop.

Just like Zoe. Probably a hoarder on the outside.

Lindsay grew up in Manhattan as the only daughter of two famous dancers. Her father was good with money and made a small fortune during the dot com boom. Having grown up wealthy, the fifty-eight-year-old woman had led a life of privilege. She'd spent summers in Europe and attended an Ivy League college. This was not on her own merit, but on her father's contributions to the school's capital campaign. Yet with all the opportunities in the world, Lindsay had never worked a day in her life. Instead, she'd spent her father's money on marijuana and other drugs—swimming through the 70s in a sea of sex, drugs, and rock and roll.

Her kinky curly hair is a dull shade of manufactured burgundy. Only the deep wrinkles in her face give away Lindsay's age. She's already taken a liking to Tina. *Maybe it's the rainbow hair.* Lola isn't sure she likes or trusts Lindsay. She wishes the duo would decide to become roommates, leaving her a private space. But Lindsay's extensive trust fund has bought her the biggest and most well-lit room in the entire hospital. A single; as rare as a good meal at Rosewood.

Lindsay gobbles up her food and baits Tina as Lola watches.

"Maybe what we need to do is try to escape," she says. "Have you ever tried it?"

Oh, here we go again! Lola can't help but shake her head.

Tina shakes her head too, but in a different way. "Doesn't work. This place is like Alcatraz."

"…at least they have the good drugs," Lindsay says. "What you've got to do is act like your drugs aren't working so you can get more. Then it's all good and this place won't bother you."

Yeah. Just what she needs.

"I need more drugs so I can stock up," Tina says. "You got extras?"

Knows what she wants and isn't afraid to ask for it. Good. Suicidal. Not good.

"No. But it doesn't mean I can't get some. Money talks." Lindsay winks at Tina.

Edna's head springs up. She glares at Lindsay. "Fuck you, cunt! Watch your back!" she growls.

Lola literally has to cover her mouth to avoid laughing at Lindsay's startled expression while Justin begins eating his third meal.

Passionate. Good! I want that quality!

126

Lola tries it all on for feel: *I'm Lola. I'm passionate, not afraid to ask for what I want, determined, and appreciative. I'm not suicidal, stubborn, alone or anxiety ridden. Yes. That sounds good. Maria? What do you think? Does that work?*

***

Tim

It kills me how unappreciative Host can be. Typical woman, I guess. Maria would say it's natural and defend her. But I'm sick of it. I'm avoiding Maria today. She's given me enough shit to do. "Plan how she's going to survive in the real world, Tim," she said. That's what women do. They drop stuff in your lap and expect you to figure it out. Meantime, for them? It's all about feelings. Dude, I'm sick of it.

Who cares who is passionate? Who cares who is anxiety ridden? If you want to talk true anxiety, try being stuck in here with these hens. Sometimes, I think I'm gonna stroke. But that can't happen. The curse of an alter is you can't die 'til your host dies and Host is gonna live forever.

Seriously, can you imagine having to ask yourself who you are? I have no tolerance or sympathy for that shit. Just do what works for you. Be around people you like and get away from those you don't. Do shit you like to do and don't do stuff you aren't into. Is that really so hard? I need to get out of here. Frog too. Poor kid.

There are times when I think a merge might actually be the best thing for all of us. But those times come about every one in 1,000. I wonder, sometimes, if I merged with all this estrogen, would I be absorbed into their pink cloud and disappear? I might be happier in a merge. But there's no way I can let myself think that way. It would be like losing a fight. Ya gotta go down swingin', right?

Maria's got me trying to figure out a plan to survive if we get out of here but I don't see what the big deal is. Host would go to her halter mother's house. It's not like halter mom wouldn't take care of everything. And I think that's what's got Maria so worried. If halter mom is on the scene and doing everything for Host, what will Maria do? I need to remind Maria she will still have the younger alters to worry about. Maybe that will shut her up. Maybe if I tell her letting Host leave without a plan is like letting your kid go to college. Host has to learn to make her own mistakes. But Maria won't work that way.

She expects spreadsheets and timelines and shit. Enter me, Tim, at your service!

If I was like Maria, I'd get Rabbit on this. She's as good as anyone with planning. But I'm not sure jumping off the Golden Gate Bridge is the kind of plan Maria's looking for. Rabbit's not a bad kid. I get why she's depressed and shit. It's got to be hard being an adolescent in here. She'll grow out of it. She's the one I worry about most. If she does something stupid—like her cutting—and hurts Host, we're all in trouble. Maria's freaked Host can't handle her mother? Open your eyes, lady! Rabbit may snap any day now and try to kill Host, and us, for real. But no one listens to me. Maria just laughs when I try to warn her about that.

So, if I were to pretend halter mom wasn't going to do everything for Host, I guess I'd have to start with the basics: food, shelter, housing, medications. But even in that situation, the halter doctor and staff here would set Host up in a halfway house or something, right? So what does Maria want? I don't get it. Host doesn't need a plan. What Host needs is the balls to carry this out and get out of here. And balls? Well, there aren't many of those in here, unfortunately. The next alter better be a boy. If we're gonna be stuck in here, we at least need to balance this shit out.

Chapter Eleven:
Digging Deeper

"Are you *sure* you're ready for this?" Dr. Hillcrest asks for the sixth time.

Ask two more times and you will have officially asked every single one of us, Lola thinks. "Yes, I'm sure."

"And you've talked to the others, right?"

"Yes. All of them."

"How are they feeling about this?"

"They're fine with it, I promise," Lola lies. There's no need to tell him the alters never completely agree on anything. *He should know that anyway*, she justifies. *More than half. The majority. Close enough. That's all we need to make a decision.*

"Okay. So what we will do—I'll hypnotize you and then ask for each of the alters to come forward. We'll do it in order of age. If I feel like they're struggling, I'll bring you back. But I need you to promise that you won't disappear on us," he says. "Stay close, Lola."

"I understand. They understand. Stop worrying," Lola assures him. "Maria's already ready."

"Okay, just let me make sure this video is ready to go and we'll get started. I'm really proud of you."

"Thanks." Hypnosis isn't something Lola's sure she believes in. But she trusts Dr. Hillcrest—to a point—and wants to do anything that will make the alters happy, get them all out of here, and mostly shut them up.

Moments later, Lola watches the scene before her play out almost as if it were a movie. She knows the main character is her but cannot completely connect with Dr. Hillcrest's words. For a moment, she has second thoughts. But she won't stop this: *You will have plenty of time to process it later. Go easy and trust Dr. Hillcrest. Maria says this is the best way to go.* She blinks lightly as the world around her begins to flutter away into a sea of anguish. Memories of her past run over her in waves. And before she knows it, she is back inside herself.

***

"Maria?"

"Yes, hello, Halt—I mean, Dr. Hillcrest. It's nice to see you again. How have you been?"

"I'm well, Maria. How are you?"

"I'm doing okay. We all are, in fact. We're excited that you and Host—Lola— have agreed to let us talk to you. It will be nice for everyone to get a chance," Maria says, praying the others will go along with this game. *Don't think about Clare.*

"I know you are a leader in there. I'm wondering how you feel about a merge. Have you talked to Lola about that?" Dr. Hillcrest stares at his client—one of eight in the same body.

Maria can only assume he's searching for answers. "Yes. Alters aren't like humans, Dr. Hillcrest. We understand it's in Lola's best interest. We're okay with whatever makes her better. Alters aren't selfish. We only, truly, want what's best for Host."

Dr. Hillcrest nods, jotting on his clipboard. "And you all feel this way?"

"Yup. All of us." Maria bites Host's lip. "Is that all? Tim's here if you want to talk to him."

"That would be fine," Dr. Hillcrest says. "Thanks for coming."

***

"Hey Doc," Tim says. "So, yeah, I'm okay with it too. A merge will be a cool adventure." *If you're buying that you're an idiot. No straight guy is ever going to be okay with being stuck in a woman's body. Ever.*

"Are you sure? Lola mentioned there might be some resistance from you and Frog, being guys and all," Dr. Hillcrest says.

Tim thinks carefully before choosing his words; Maria may have already done damage with her slips. "Here's the thing, though. I'm already in a woman's body, right? So what's the difference, really?"

Dr. Hillcrest nods, scribbling. "I'm not sure. I guess I'd worry about permanence? Once a personality has merged, the alters generally don't separate again."

Tim shrugs. "And that's okay too. Listen, Doc. You gotta realize that this isn't an easy life, being an alter. So my feeling is, what can be worse than the situation we're in now? Do you realize we are sharing less than eight square feet of space in here?"

Dr. Hillcrest sighs. "I can't imagine that would be easy."

"Trust me, it's not. Who do you want to talk to next? Anything else you need, Doc?"

"Do you have any questions for me? There's no rush for you to leave. We haven't had a lot of time together," Dr. Hillcrest says.

If Tim had any plan at all to actually merge, he'd have a million questions. *Come up with something, so he doesn't suspect,* Tim thinks. He pauses. "Well, I do worry how Hos—Lola—will get alone in the outside world. What is the plan once this is all fixed and she's able to leave Rosewood?" *God dammit. I'm just like Maria. Fix it!* "She's been in here, locked up, for 10,938 days. That's 262,512 hours and 15,750,720 minutes, give or take. Don't you think that's long enough?"

"That's a great question. And wow! She said you're good with numbers, but that's great! Did you just do that in your head?"

Tim shrugs, unsure how to answer.

Dr. Hillcrest doesn't push. "Okay, well, it's a great question. It's one I've been talking to her mother—Stella—quite extensively about. Apparently, her mother is fine with her moving back into her house. We plan to have her in an intensive partial hospitalization program with daily group sessions and someone to monitor her medications for the first few months," Dr. Hillcrest says. "We don't send anyone out there without a plan or set them up to fail. We have a whole transition team who will work on this."

***

"Finally!" Clare pulls Host's hair from the tight bun on the top of her head. Brown hair spills over her shoulders and Clare looks around Dr. Hillcrest's office for any sign of a mirror. "They *never* let *me* talk! How are you doing, Doc? It's been awhile!"

"Hello Clare." Dr. Hillcrest smiles.

"So what did ya want to see me for? Something about a merge?" Clare silently tells Maria and Tim to shut up. She knows what she's doing. *If you two keep acting like I'm an idiot, I'll be one and fuck up your whole plan, so stop! I want out of here more than ya'll combined, you fools!*

"Well, yes, basically…"

"Bring it! I can handle anything. Like Tim says, total adventure, Doc. And I'm always up for a new challenge."

"But Clare, it's not that simple. Do you understand what a merge is?" Dr. Hillcrest asks.

"Yeah. You—nice tie! Love it! Great color on ya! Sweet like a peach!"

"Thank you, Clare, continue."

"A merge is where you all come together and form one personality. Right?"

"Yes. But that means Clare, as you know yourself, will be part of a larger personality."

"Like larger than life?" Clare asks.

"Well, I'm not sure what the main personality will look like after a merge. But I'm sure there will be quite a bit of Clare in there." Dr. Hillcrest laughs.

"Exactly! So what's the big deal? A merge means I can be part of the main personality *and* finally get Host—sorry— 'Lola,' to get off her butt and make something of herself! Ya'll worry too much! This will be great!"

***

"I mean, it wouldn't be so bad—Hang on! I don't know why Clare insists on having her hair all over the place..."—Zoe pulls Lola's hair into a messy twist on top of her head— "...there!—It wouldn't be so bad if there weren't so many of us. I just don't understand how we're supposed to just merge and suddenly be one Host?" Zoe grasps the plan to make Dr. Hillcrest believe they are all on board with a merge but refuses to have her questions left unanswered. "How is it going to work?"

137

"I understand all of your fears and frustrations. It's a scary thing to think about, for sure. But what I can assure you is I have seen it happen quite successfully many times." Dr. Hillcrest looks Zoe in the eye. "I think you will all be glad in the end."

"Okay, but you haven't answered my questions. "How does it work? Like it or not, believe it or not, we aren't the same person, I want kids, for example! Host doesn't!" *Shut up so I can hear the halter, Maria and Tim. I do have a right to know these things too!*

"I think those kinds of bigger decisions will become easier when you are all the same person," Dr. Hillcrest says. "But the question of how the personalities actually merge is easier. Each of you was born to help Lola deal with a certain emotion, circumstance or time in her life, right?"

Zoe nods, but crosses her arms over her chest.

"So the way it works is we begin looking at those emotions and situations and begin recovery for each of you. Let's start with an obvious example. Clare came about when Holly was killed, right?" Dr. Hillcrest asks.

Zoe nods. "Right."

"So to make Clare comfortable with a merge, we need for Clare and for Lola to be okay with Holly's death. In Lola's case, she needs to stop thinking it was her fault when clearly it wasn't. And Clare needs to know that Lola is okay without a best friend so that she can be free to stop trying to make everything okay in the world and make people happy. Clare needs to know that it's okay to grieve, and frankly? So does Lola," Dr. Hillcrest says.

"So basically, it's by helping each one of us that we can help Lola?"

"Yes, basically."

"Okay, what about me then? No one seems to know why I even came around. I think Host just likes collecting things. And there's nothing wrong with that. But you can't fix what isn't broken."

"Good point. Do you think Lola's not broken?"

"Oh, she's broken all right," Zoe says. "We all are. If you really think about it, she's holding us hostage in here. So, yeah, she's broken. I just wish you luck in trying to fix it—us—all."

Dr. Hillcrest laughs. "Gee, thanks…but that is plan, Zoe. I think it will work, eventually. The meds alone will help. They are helping, from what I understand…"

***

"Hi Frog, thanks for coming to see me," Dr. Hillcrest says.

Tim made me. "No prob."

"So you know why you're here today, right?"

Frog looks at the floor, trying to remember his script. *I suck at this.* "Yup."

"Could you share with me why you think you're here?"

Fuck. "Because you want us all to merge so we can leave here?" Frog looks at the camera and it's blinking red light. No one warned him Dr. Hillcrest was recording. *Great.*

"Sort of. Can you share more?"

"I don't know what else you want me to say. You want us here so we can merge."

"How do you feel about a merge?"

"I'm cool with it."

"I feel like there's something you aren't telling me. Is there anything else you'd like to say?"

"No."

"Well, how have things been for you? It can't be easy in there with all those women. Tim says it's hell…"

"It's fine. I stick to myself and read a lot."

"What are you readying these days?"

"Right now, *The Prince*."

"Awww, a great book! What do you think of it?"

Frog's face lights up. "I like it. I think of it as a how-not to rule. It cracks me up because it reminds me of Tim and Maria."

Dr. Hillcrest laughs. "Sometimes, the best books are the ones we can see our reflections in."

"What book would be your reflection?" Frog asks, suddenly more serious.

"Oh, gosh. That's a hard one. I'm going to have to think about that. I will get back to you for sure."

Typical. "Sounds good. So are we all set?" Frog asks, desperate to get off the hot seat. He cracks his knuckles. Pop. Crack. Pop. "Basically whatever Maria and Tim think is fine with me. I trust them."

"Despite their way of leading?"

Pop. Pop. Frog laughs. "They mean well. And that counts for a lot."

"Yes, I suppose it does."

***

"Okay, Sam, I want you to draw a picture of yourself on this piece of paper. But the trick is that I need you to do it with

141

your right hand. Can you do that for me, Samantha?"

"But I'm left-handed."

"That's okay. That's what makes this game fun," Dr. Hillcrest says.

"Okay, I'll try," Samantha says in a child's voice, reaching for a crayon with her left hand but switching it to her right. "This feels so weird. Did Zoe do this too?"

"No, Zoe wanted me to save the best game for you."

Samantha smiles, presses the purple crayon to the page, and begins to draw. She looks up at Dr. Hillcrest. "Can I draw Peter Pan?"

***

Lola rubs her eyes, surprised to discover a crayon in her hand, as she wakes up in Dr. Hillcrest's office. His voice sounds like it's coming from the other end of a long tunnel and she can't tell if he's walking toward her or away.

"With me?" he asks.

She isn't ready to answer him. Unsure of what he's even asking, she puts the crayon on the small table in front of her and leans back into the plush couch.

"Take your time," he persists, as though he has a choice in the matter.

Lola remembers why she's here. She'd allowed him to hypnotize her to bring the alters to the surface. Panic grips at her stomach as she considers what they may have told him. She glances at a crumpled piece of green construction paper on the table. On it, is a primitive stick drawing of a child with a huge U-shaped smile and large brown eyes in a Peter Pan costume. It reminds her of something Sam would have drawn at about the age of four. Next to it, on red paper, is a picture of a car with bold orange flames coming out of it. And beside that are several wads of used tissues next to an empty Kleenex box. *What did he do to her?*

Lola snaps to attention, instantly defensive of her youngest alter.

"Is Sam okay?"

"Yes, they all are, don't worry," Dr. Hillcrest says. "Everyone was great. It was nice seeing—"

"Why was she crying?"

"Lola, she is okay, I promise you. You will be able to see the tapes from the sessions another day. They will help you," Dr. Hillcrest reassures his client. "Right now, we need to focus on you being okay and getting you fully back with us. Your session ran long today for obvious reasons and you must be starving and need a break."

On cue, Lola's stomach begins to rumble. She looks to the clock on Dr. Hillcrest's desk, which reads 1:08 p.m. *Great. We missed lunch. Clare will be thrilled but Frog has got to be losing his mind.*

"Yes, actually. I'm feeling sort of hungry. Can you tell me what happened, though?"

"I really think that's best saved for another day. You've worked hard and need to rest your mind. I can call Paul and ask if they have any bagged lunches left in the kitchen and have him bring one with him when he comes to collect you, if you'd like?"

Lola nods.

"I do want to share with you that I spent time convincing each of the alters that if they hope to merge—which they all insisted they did—they are going to have to cooperate with one another. The only one I didn't speak with about that was Sam, but she and I did other work together that I found very helpful," Dr. Hillcrest says. "All of this I will share with you, I promise."

Lola nods again. *There's no way they all want to merge. They're all lying to you,*

you fool. There is no planet on which Tim and Frog are going to be okay with being a woman forever. And there's even less of a chance of shutting Clare and Zoe down. Too strong. Too strong for me, even. And I'm the one whose supposed to be in charge.

***

Clare

Okay, seriously. I mean let's be realistic, ya'll. I honestly rocked that hypno hocus pocus, didn't I? You can hold your applause, but I don't know what Tim and Maria were worried about. They're the ones who kept screwing up, not this chick! Hell, Zoe's supposed to be the actress and I did a heck of a lot better than her, don't ya think? Here's the thing. I want Host out of this place more than anyone. A merge? That will never happen. For one, I'm Host's BFF. A girl doesn't abandon her BFF. I'm not Host's halter father, ya'll. I'm Clare! Large, in charge. And here to stay! How many more times do I need to say it before they get it?

You guys ever hear of Tig? Famous comedian. Had cancer. Had awful life. Her mother died like a week after she got diagnosed. Had to have her boobs cut off, ya'll. Host would die. I'd die for her. We'd be running to a cosmetic surgeon. Give that Tig a lot of credit. But anyway, Tig was okay as a comic. But then, when cancer struck, she hit it big. Why? Because she had the balls to joke about her life and her tragedies. My goal? I'm gonna get Host out of here and make her a millionaire. I figure, with her life, we have more material and tragedy than Tig could ever dream up. We're gonna make Tig's cancer like a blip on the comedic stage. People like to laugh. But they like to laugh at real shit more than anything. Host's got very real shit.

Ya gotta capitalize on what you've got. It's simple. You don't have a lot when you've spent so many years locked up. But what you *do* get in a nuthouse is more crazy stories and scenarios than any halter on the outside. The problem is, being locked up, there's no way to get your material out there.

Once we get out of here, I'm gonna do a set that will blow people's minds. I've already got Host changing her appearance. Taught her how to do makeup myself. Got her on the treadmill three days a week. Have her watching what she eats. Tig's no fat chick. Then again, maybe a fat chick is funny?

I'm even going to Holly. Yeah, sounds mean, right. But think about the material in that. Get them in the heart. No need to act like there was a merge on the outside, right? I can literally do a set on how I'm jealous of Holly who gets to be her forever BFF simply because she died. It's not like Host has to listen to it. Screw what Maria says. She's too protective anyway. I can make it funny as hell: Being jealous of a dead BFF sixteen-year-old ghost. Can you see it?

There's comedy in everything. It's how we survive. At least people like us. I don't know why no one wants to admit it. Ya'll should have seen me after the accident, making Host laugh. No head injury was going to shut me up. I was there for that girl. And I'm not going anywhere. It's payback time. Clare's time. My time to shine. I don't care if I have to do it as an alter. Honestly? I'd love to be the main personality. I think Host would let me do it too. But we aren't there yet. For now, if I have to live for Friday nights, that's what I'll do. I can see my name in lights now, can't you?

Chapter Twelve:
Taking Turns

"Look, whether it's fake or not, we may have a true merge coming up. I think the least we deserve is one day—just one—where we can each be in charge. No other voices judging us or telling us what to do. There are seven of us. It would only take a week," Tim says. "Come on, Host, please? Those meds make me nervous. You're already having trouble hearing us."

"Don't pressure her. If she doesn't want to do it, let it go," Maria says.

"No, it's okay. We can try that. I mean, think of it this way, if they see me as seven different people—a different person each day—I can say it's intentional. I can say it's to resolve each of the personalities before a merge. Do you think they'd buy it?" Host asks, feeling like a referee but remembering what Dr. Hillcrest said about recovery and each alter needing a cure of their own.

"I think that's a great way to spin it. My worry is Clare," Maria says. "She can't get us in trouble. We'll let her do it but we'll need to keep a close eye on her."

"What we do is have Clare do her day on the day of the talent show. She'll be quiet until show time, working on her set." Frog jumps in as the voice of reason.

"Great thinking! Where is she? Has anyone even seen her? Why does she think she doesn't need to be at meetings?" Maria asks.

Rabbit shrugs. "She thinks they're stupid."

"Who cares if she's here? At least she did okay with the halter doc," Tim says.

"Okay, guys, I don't have a lot of time. So that's the plan? A week? You each get a turn?"

"Works for us. Anyone want to vote?" Maria asks.

"No voting!" Tim and Frog holler in unison. "Let's just get this done, we don't have much time with this," Tim says. "You're first, Maria. So make it count. We've gotta start today and you won't get as much time as the rest if we're going to land Clare on the right day for the talent show. Are you cool with that?"

"Yes," Maria answers. "It's not like my day will be any different than Host's. The halters won't even know it's me."

"On my day, I'm gonna eat ice cream all day long!" Samantha shouts.

"Oh, God, don't tell Clare that!" Zoe warns. "She'll make us do the elliptical machine all day long!"

***

Maria isn't sure she likes being the only one in charge of Host's body any more than she likes being in charge of the other alters. It's not how she pictured it. Main personalities, or hosts, have more responsibilities than she'd considered. *How am I supposed to watch what the alters are up to when I'm stuck dealing with halters? Maybe this was a bad idea.* For starters, there's the mandatory afternoon group therapy session. She doesn't like being told what to do and resists when the group therapist tries to make her speak about her feelings.

"I'm not really sure what that has to do with anything," she says, when asked how she feels about group interactions. "I'm supposed to be working on fixing myself and talking about how I feel about other people seems like a waste of time."

The therapist leans into the circle, urging Maria to disclose her feelings on Lindsay and Tina's ways of communicating with the group. "The way we experience other people often tells us a lot about ourselves," she says.

Maria stares at the woman's thick glasses. She wants to take them off her face and wipe them down.

"I feel like Lindsay and Tina do just fine communicating," she finally says.

"Normally, you don't like when there's conflict in the group," the therapist pushes. "Are you feeling okay today?"

"Yes. I'm feeling fine. I don't think anyone likes conflict. I just don't see how pointing out other people's flaws would reduce conflict," Maria says, hoping the therapist will let it go.

Instead, she's saved by Tina. "She's not mean like you and everyone else here," the young girl says. "Leave her alone. She's got enough to deal with. Dr. Hillcrest is trying to fix her and get her out of here. Ask her about her feelings on that instead."

The therapist flips through her clipboard. "I hadn't heard anything about that. Is this true, Lola?"

Maria doesn't answer, forgetting she's in Host's body and supposed to answer to the name Lola.

"Lola?"

"Well, answer her, idiot! She's not going to let it go. Just tell her you're psyched to get out of here already so we can be done," Lindsay says.

"Maybe she doesn't want to leave," Justin says, kicking his legs into the center of the circle. "This place isn't that bad. There's pretty girls here."

"I'm fine with leaving. I'm fine with staying. I'm trying not to think about it," Maria says, remembering how indecisive Host can be. *You've got to do a better job with this. You've got to get to those letters.*

Maria manages to make it through the rest of group session and dinner without anyone discovering her total takeover of the host body. When she finally returns to Host's room for free time, she scrambles to her bed and pulls the large manila folder from under the mattress. From what she can tell, about ten of the sixty or so letters have been read. All letters that come into the hospital are screened in the mail room and have been technically opened. But there's a difference between a letter opener slice in the top of a letter and one that's been looked at more closely. Thankfully, the mail room puts a sticker over the slice, which helps Maria determine what Host has and hasn't read. She quickly skims the content of the letters she's sure Host has read. *Thank God for small favors. She can't know too much if she's only read these.*

152

Swallowing the knot of guilt she feels in the pit of her stomach, she scans the room for a place to hide the letters. But in a place where they do daily inspections and have strict rules about hiding anything, she can't find an obvious spot.

Maria shoves the thick, larger envelope up Host's shirt and walks down the hall. She keeps her eyes to the ground and moves quickly to a dayroom. There, she spots a paper recycling bin and quickly pushes the envelope and thirty years of communication from Stella into the bottom of the trash. *It's Wednesday night. They recycle on Thursdays. It's the best thing for her. For us,* she tells herself, and returns to her room. *When Host finds out, I'll just deny, deny, deny.*

***

What the heck was Maria griping about? Is that a woman thing? It's great being in charge! If I can only avoid the bathroom, this is gonna be a great day. What day is this, anyway? Wednesday? No, Wednesday was doc.

Tim sits in Lola's body across from Justin in full control of Host's body Thursday morning at breakfast. When

Justin reaches for Tim's orange, he swats the young man's hand away.

"Did I say you could have my orange?" he asks.

Justin stares at Tim. "You always let me have your orange. You told me to stop askin' and just take it."

Tina looks up from her jagged cuticles. "What gives? You always let him eat your shit."

"I'm just hungry today, no big deal," Tim says, realizing he's putting up red flags but not willing to give up the fruit. Being an alter, you never get first dibs on the taste buds unless you happen to be in the right place at the right time.

Tina rolls her eyes at Tim and nudges Lindsay.

Lindsay ignores her, grumbling under her breath about why anyone would eat hospital food in the first place.

"Here, have mine," Tina says, handing her orange to Justin.

Justin uncrosses his arms to take the orange and glares at Tim.

"You're mean. You're a promise breaker and I don't like you anymore. You can't be our friend and you can't sit at our table," he says.

"I didn't know you owned the table, dude," Tim says. "Chill out."

"This is our table and it has been way before you got put in here. Before that you were too crazy to even eat at the tables and had to eat in your room." Justin puts Tina's orange on his tray and crosses his arms again. "Go sit with other mean people. Over there!" He points to a long table diagonal from the one they are sitting at. It's static plastic seats mirror the very seat Tim is sitting on.

"Dude, just eat," Tim says, rolling his eyes and biting into his own freshly pealed orange. "How long do we have before they make us do stuff?"

"Like we ever have free time? When's the next field trip?" Lindsay asks.

Tina shrugs. "There's some park thing next Saturday. But it's totally lame and there won't be shopping, so you will hate it."

"Does the park have a gift shop? And are there men there? Maybe we could find some hotties and…" Lindsay muses into the distance.

"Are we going to die?" Edna begins rocking in her seat.

"No, Edna! We aren't going to die! Not as long as Lola moves to another table with the other mean people," Justin says. He looks at Tim. "And stop calling me dude!"

"Cut it out, Justin. That's not going to help her," Tina says. "We're fine, Edna. Don't listen to him. See what you did, Lola? Just give the kid the damn fruit next time."

Wow. This place really is full of nuts, Tim surmises. Thirty years of this shit— you're mean if you don't give up your breakfast—and I'd be crazy too. Poor Host.

Twenty minutes and several attempts by Justin to get Tim to leave later, an orderly tells the crew to clean up and get ready for art therapy.

Art what? Is she serious? This is something for the chicks. Not for me. How the hell did I get stuck here on the arts and crafts day? I shoulda made Maria go today. Great. How am I going to get measurements of this place if I'm spending all my time painting?

Tim looks up from his "this is me" t-shirt project an hour later. The clock says ten a.m. He has exactly twelve hours before Clare's banging on Host's brain for her turn. *I shouldn't have wasted the night sleeping. Clare would have been the overtired one, not me. I've wasted so much time. By the time the end of the day gets here, I'm going to have fought with a nut over an orange and made a stupid t-*

shirt Host will never wear because it has a picture of a bodyguard on it. This is so stupid. I want a do over.

***

The next evening, Clare—in full control of Lola's body—steps on a makeshift stage in the hospital cafeteria without a care in the world. She tosses Host's hair and surmises her audience before speaking, smiling. Finally, after a mental count of audience members—*200 or so? Not bad*—she pulls the microphone from its stand.

"Hi. I'm Clare. Most of you know me as 'the fun one.'" She pauses as she flamboyantly flips Host's hair and crosses Host's eyes. "But let me tell ya'll, it ain't that fun sharing this—" she looks down at Host's body, dressed in a burlap sack, literally, found by Zoe, and does a 360 degree turn "—body."

The audience laughs, ignoring Edna's "Are we gonna die?"

"No, seriously. Ya'll know what I'm talking about. How many of you hear the voices too? Don't be shy. How many of you have alters—more fashionable ones, prettier, smarter, smoooooother on the eyes—in you too? Let's have a show of hands for the identity disorders, skitzos, and MPDs in the audience tonight!"

About a third the people in the room stand or raise their hands. Others, family members, staff, friends, laugh.

"'Cause it can't be easy being a host, either, ya'll," Clare continues after the hands go down. "Now, let's get a round of applause for the peeps like us who—if we could ever get out of this nuthouse, would walk into a fancy restaurant, look at the hostess, and say "Lola, party of eight."

A group in the back clap and cheer, yelling, "Tom, party of ten!" and "Woot, woot!"

"'Cause it ain't easy, I tell ya'll. And sometimes, a girl just *has* to run naked down the halls to get any attention around here."

***

Zoe has a plan by the time her turn comes around on Saturday. With many of the residents off on a park field trip, it'll be easy to get her hands on things she's been eying all week. She zips through breakfast, offering her orange to Justin before he asks for it and reassuring Edna before she needs it. By noon, she chomps on her bag lunch in the hospital atrium, waiting for the right moment to make her move. She throws half of her bologna sandwich in the garbage, wipes her face with the back of her hand, and walks toward the largest dayroom.

It takes a total of three hours for Zoe to collect precisely 28 items—all on her list. *A lot more effective with my time than Tim was during his time in charge!* She wants to squeal in delight as she stuffs dozens of treasures—pens, pencils, paper, stuffed animals, electronics, plastic utensils, pillows, blankets, and a picture frame— from around the hospital into one of Lindsay's spare closets. She stays quiet, it's not time to celebrate just yet. She can't get caught. *No one will ever find this stuff in here. She shouldn't get a private room anyway. And it's what she gets for going on a field trip just to find a man. Slut! Just like Clare; running around naked for attention. Sam and Rabbit are going to be so happy when I give them their new things. I'm the best sister alter ever!* She hugs a box of crayons to her chest before tucking it behind a pile of extra blankets, closing the door, and sneaking back to Host's room. *Best day ever!*

***

Zoe

I don't know where Maria's head's at, but lucky for Sam, I'm with the program. Sure, you may judge me. I know it's wrong to steal. But I can't help myself. I look at this seven-year-old girl and all I want to do is give her things. If I could, I'd give her a body so she could be a host. Normally, Maria's on this kind of thing but I think she's distracted with the merge. Sam's birthday is only a month away and we need to be prepared. We haven't gotten her anything. We forgot Rabbit too. I'll fix that. Some mother figure Maria is, huh?

Host had to do a therapy exercise last week on money and things. I think they decided to do that because of halter Lindsay. Either way, the exercise was to pretend you had a million dollars. You had to buy each person on the list something. I was thinking about that when I stole stuff from the dayroom and other people's rooms. If I had a million dollars, I'd buy Sam anything to make her happy. I know what it's like to spend your whole life locked up in this place. I know what it's like to have things constantly taken away—usually it's because stupid Clare has done something wrong again. I'm tired of seeing Sam hurt. So before you judge me, realize that I'm doing this for Sam.

Yeah, I got a few things for me too. So what? It's not the end of the world.

What *will* be the end of the world is if this pretend merge and us getting out of here doesn't happen. I hope Tim and Maria know what they're doing. I want Host out of here so we can start our lives. I'm hoping to meet a gorgeous prince charming. I love to steal books—romance novels—and that's exactly what I'm looking for in my own real life. I don't care if they say fairy tales can't come true. I don't believe it. They also say alters aren't real. What a joke! I know for a *fact* they're lying about *that*. So the halters can kiss my ass about fairy tales and happy endings. Host is going to get hers. I'm going to get mine. The rest of us too. That's all there is to it. Maybe we can find another host to marry with multiple personalities and everyone could be happy. Sure, it might get complicated. Think of the drama! But how is it different, than, say polygamy? Heck, I bet they even make dating pages for people with more than one personality. It could be really interesting. That Tina girl says the Internet has everything. Why not?

Clare's driving me nuts. She's running around trying to come up with slogans for her first show on the outside. If anyone's going to hit the big stage, it's me. Not her. I've had a plan for a lot longer than her and I'm not mean like her—making fun of Host and Host's life. Some best friend she is.

Honestly? Lately? They are all driving me nuts. Soon I'll have alters of my own out of pure necessity. I need to be with like minds. We can call them sub-alters. Tim's right about one thing. It's too small in here. I know Host's trying. I really do. I just wish she'd move a little faster. It's been long enough. We're ready. We want out. We're tired of being held hostage.

Chapter Thirteen:
Round Two

"I'm *so* proud of you, Lola! Dr. Hillcrest said you've made great progress! I *know* this can't be easy on you. I only wish they'd changed your meds years ago. We've missed *so* much time," Stella hangs her head, giving Frog a chance to come up with a response to Host's halter mother. But Stella's so anxious to spend time with her daughter that he doesn't even need to. She continues, barely stopping to inhale. "You know, I was thinking, on the day you get out, we could all get together—the whole family. Travis says it might be too much but I guess we can decide that later. Charlotte really misses you and I can't wait to see what you think of her kids, Will and Aubree. I wrote you about them, remember?"

Frog nods. *Holy cow. She's manic or something. Is this woman always this way? No wonder Maria hates her. Take a chill pill, lady.*

"Will is *such* a kicker. He reminds me of a little monkey sometimes. So much energy. I remember when you were that way. *So* full of life," Stella sighs, looking around the hospital atrium. Her eyes land on Edna, who rocks, alone in a corner, staring at a blank wall. "Is she okay?"

Frog laughs, thinking, about how many times a day the woman herself asks that question. "She's fine."

Stella leans forward and whispers, "Why is *she* here? She's *my* age."

Point at her, why don't ya? Frog shrugs. "She thinks she's gonna die."

Stella blinks rapidly, eying the old woman. She whispers even softer, "But we're all going to die, Lola. Do you remember Mr. Schromen? He died just last week. Poor old guy. Brought the paper to my door every day for years, as if Travis didn't even exist. He was a hoot! Oh, never mind. You don't care about that stuff. Has that doctor told you when you're coming home?"

Frog shakes his head. "Nope."

"How long has she—that woman—been here?"

"No clue."

"Are you okay, Dragonfly? You've barely said two words today," Stella asks, her brow twisting and her eyes finally off Edna.

"I'm good." *Dragonfly? Gross. Insects are worse than amphibians. Who would want a nickname like that?*

"I'm your *mother*. I know something's not right. Have they messed with your meds again? You seem bored or something, I can't quite put my finger on it."

"I'm good, I swear," Frog pushes a stray hair that's fallen in Host's face away quickly. *I'm in hell. Can you tell that too, Ma? And by the way, you aren't* my *mother.*

"Well, I've done all the talking. And you must get sick of talking about this place and the people in it. Tell me, what would *you* like to talk about?"

Frog smiles. He can't help himself. He pauses and then, "In your opinion, do you think that a thunderstorm is nature's sexual innuendo?"

Stella gasps.

***

Rabbit stares at Tina early the next morning in Lola's body. The girl's stringy, colorful hair and smudged eyeliner make her look like she's just been caught in a rainstorm. But in fact, the young adult is sleeping peacefully in the shared room. *Is that how I'd look if I was allowed to have my own body? Would my cuts look like that too?*

She winces as deep voices travel down the Rosewood hall, under the door, and into the room. She wants time to figure Tina out. Time is something she doesn't have a lot of, especially on a Monday. Rabbit holds her breath as Tina rolls over, facing the wall, and adjusts her pillow. Her arms are more exposed now and Rabbit can finally make out her tattoo by squinting. It reads "perseverance" in an Algerian font and it's flanked on either side with tiny hawks. One hawk, the one at the end of the word, looks like his head's been cut off, then sewed back on and held there by the long scar that runs five inches down Tina's arm like a ghost. Rabbit checks Host's arms in the dim light coming from a dingy window: Nothing but tiny freckles. But she knows better. Rabbit cuts where no one can see. She isn't as brave—*or attention seeking?*—as Host's roommate.

Rabbit turns her attention to the bland night table to the left of Tina's bed. She wishes she could remember where Tina kept her iPod. She'd been hoping to get her hands on Tina's playlist—music she's sure to love. She looks around the room, knowing it must be somewhere. Tina never goes anywhere without her music.

166

Tina's sudden squawking scares her out of her thoughts. "Are you just going to stare at me and my shit or what? Maybe you need more meds, dude. Why aren't you sleeping?" Tina rubs her eyes and glares at Rabbit.

"I'm—I'm sorry. I was just—"

"Dude! What time is it? You're never up early. What are you doing? How am I supposed to sleep with you staring at me?"

"I'm sorry. It's four—"

"Four in the morning? How long have you been staring at me like a freak? Take a picture, it lasts longer. Geesh!"

"I just couldn't sleep."

"Then go get a nurse or something. Get some meds. But leave me out of it. I can barely handle this dump *with* rest. I need all the sleep I can get. I was having a great dream too and you ruined it!"

"I'm sorry," Rabbit says again.

"It's fine," Tina concedes. "I can't believe I lost my fucking iPod. I can't sleep without music. That's not helping me."

"Yeah, I was wondering about that. I never see you without it—"

"Hello! I already asked you about it. If you'd seen it. You know it's missing. Why would you be wondering about it?"

"I'm sorry, I can't remember you asking. My brain isn't working right."

"Well, everyone's missing shit. I'm telling myself I lost it because if I think someone stole it I'm gonna kill people and that won't really get me out of here any faster, now, will it?"

Rabbit laughs, shaking her head. "No, probably not. But who would steal it?"

"Do you think that person would be alive if I *knew*? Likely not. Murder suicide is what that would be. I'd say Lindsay but let's face it, she'd just have her parents send her one if that's what she wanted. Hell, I think she asked them for a man last time she saw them. Surprised they haven't sent her one of those yet."

Is this what it's like to have a friend? Laughing feels nice and Rabbit wishes she could find Tina's iPod, to make her realize someone, anyone, cares. *Maybe then suicide wouldn't be on her mind all the time.* "I'll help you find it," she mutters. *I just need more time. But I have all day…*

*　　　　　　* * *

"I didn't steal anything! Why do you keep blaming me?" Samantha yells at Paul only an hour into her turn at the helm, who has asked for the fifth time today whether

168

or not she "borrowed" several of the items missing at Rosewood. "Ask someone else! Because it wasn't me and you're making me mad!"

"Listen, Lola, you need to stay calm. I'm not accusing you. I'm just saying that stuff went missing when everyone was on that field trip. It was only you and a handful of others who stayed behind so I thought you might have seen something," Paul explains. "It's been days and nothing's turned up. The stuff has to be in here somewhere."

"First of all, my name is *Sam*! Stop calling me Lola," Samantha puts her hand over her mouth the moment she realizes they've escaped by the shocked look on Paul's face. She tries to recover, "Kidding. Geesh. You can't even take a joke!"

But Paul's worked at Rosewood for longer than he'd care to admit and has seen this sort of thing in identity disorder patients before. "Are you okay, Lola?" he asks.

"I'm fine. I'm just tired of people acting like I stole something. I told you ten times to search my room. Search all the rooms! It's fine with me because I have nothing to hide. I'm sick of being blamed."

***

Frog

Maria and Tim said I can talk to you uncensored. My feelings on a merge or no merge and crap. They say it will be good for me. So, look out! It's Frog, Uncensored! Grab some popcorn, folks. And don't tell Clare. But seriously, I'm not sure I buy it—that they won't yell at me for speaking my mind—but it's worth a shot. I mean, I did scare Host's mom off quite successfully. That halter can sure be annoying. But she's no different than Maria, I guess. Let's see if it scares you too—the real me. It's not that I try to scare anyone. I guess they just don't expect it to come from me. Maybe it's because I'm a guy. Or maybe it's my age. The women in here seem to think we guys are dumb. I've got nothing to lose.

Anyway, do you want to know what I really think is funny about the outside world? No, I haven't been out there, but I do enough reading. And hopefully, we'll be out there soon enough. My feeling is that the world is so full of self-important halters that think they're so smart. It seems as though halters, when they reach a certain age or education level, forget how to just live and it's sad. Part of living is

170

learning, and that is what makes life so great. You think you're so smart, but you're really stupid.

Socrates said, "The only real wisdom is knowing that you know nothing." Do you know what that means? In this universe, right? Hell, even in Host's head, there is so much that we don't know and we don't understand. Where wise men thousands of years ago saw magic, we see science and if you can't understand it you hate it and you spit on it until you can't ignore it. Maybe that's why I'm here? I need to be wise enough to influence you people to realize that you know nothing at all. And there's nothing wrong with that. I just need to find a way to do this as a halter, not an alter trapped in a chick body.

While I am stuck, I want to learn as much as I can. Asking myself these questions and thinking about this all the time is what makes me who I am and I love being who I am. Will I be this same person in…ten years? Fifteen years? Twenty years? I really don't know. I hope that I am, but somehow, not as an alter. And that's why I hate the idea of a merge. Once we merge, there is no more me. No Frog. Just a 'we.' And I don't like it. Not one bit.

Yeah, this is the kind of stuff that I think about. That's why I love philosophy because it never ends, you know? You can keep asking questions and your answers just make more questions which is pretty amazing. Why am I here in this universe? Why do I exist? To ask questions, answer questions, and ask more questions. It's all over the place, man, and exciting as all hell. The chaos, the unknown, the never knowing if you're truly right or wrong, keeps you guessing and keeps you humble; because you don't know a damn thing. I guess I love that, thrive on it, you know?

Chapter Fourteen:
Second Thoughts

Dr. Hillcrest scans his notes. He's unusually quiet and Lola can't keep still as she waits for him to speak during their regular session Wednesday morning. Finally he says, "Well, you've had quite the week. I have to admit, Lola, we have some concerns. The staff has reported some things that make me think maybe you and the others just aren't ready for a merge just yet. You promised you would stay in control and do what you could to silence the others, but from the reports I'm reading…"

Oh, great. What did they do? Lola immediately regrets her decision to let the alters take turns as the main personality. She regrets more not realizing she'd have no memory whatsoever of their times in charge. "I'm not sure what you mean, Dr. Hillcrest. I have stayed in charge. I've totally ignored them and now I'm not hearing them hardly at all. The meds are working great and I feel great. I thought I had a good week," Lola fibs.

"Well, for starters, there was an art project where Ann and the therapist we brought in just for the day asked you all to create a t-shirt that defined who you are," Dr. Hillcrest says. "Do you want to explain your t-shirt?"

The last thing Lola wants to do is call on Maria for help. But what choice does she have? *Maria, hurry! What t-shirt is he talking about?* But it's Tim who answers with a "My bad, tell him you're trying to reinvent yourself and want to look brave to the world."

Lola squirms before answering. "I wanted to look brave."

Dr. Hillcrest relaxes his forehead, which had appeared tight and concerned. He scribbles on his notepad. "Oh! Interesting! I hadn't thought of that. Can you tell me more about that?"

Lola copies Tim's explanation verbatim, praying he's being serious and not playing games. But Tim's never one for games. That would be a Clare move. Tim's not a Clare. *Trust him. You don't have any other choice. He has as much to lose as you do,* she tells herself.

"Well, they asked us who we were, so I wanted people to know I was strong and in charge and able to defend myself," she says, totally unaware of why she is saying these things.

"Are you feeling particularly defensive about something? Like you need protection?" Dr. Hillcrest asks.

"No. I mean, I'm afraid, obviously, because change is coming. And that scares me. The idea of a merge is hard. I want to empower myself, if that makes sense," she says.

Dr. Hillcrest nods. "It does."

Thank God, Lola thinks, ignoring Tim's "thank *me*" in her head.

"But do you care to explain the talent show? You do realize that you went on stage as Clare. Or was that Clare?"

"Oh, no, that was me. I just wanted to, well, honor her. She'd written the entire act, so I figured it would be fun to try it out and do my best to do it for her. But, no, that was all me. It was fun, actually," Lola says, a little too convincingly. "I mean, everyone is encouraging me to figure out who I am and so I thought that trying on different, um, hats, so to speak, might be one way to do it. Ann and you have both told me that my alters are really just parts of me. So, there is Clare in me somewhere. Right?"

"But you're saying Clare wrote the set. When did she do this?"

"Oh, you know Clare, she gets so excited to perform. To make people laugh.

She did that months ago. I just tweaked it. People seemed to like it…"

"Yes. As always, Clare—you—were a hit. I can't take that away from you there," Dr. Hillcrest says, smiling.

Never again are they taking turns so that I can't remember, Lola thinks. *This is way too sticky.*

"Well, then there's your mother," Dr. Hillcrest says. "She said you acted strange during your visit. What did she mean by that?"

Whose day was Sunday? Rabbit? No. Frog. Tim, get Frog! "How do you mean, strange? I felt fine."

"She didn't really elaborate. She just left a voice message. I haven't had time to call her back yet. I thought maybe you had finally gone through more of the letters."

The letters! How could I forget about the letters? Too much going on. Do it later. I'm going to kill these guys. This is too much. No wonder I'm crazy.

"No. I mean, sure, I've read some of the letters, but so far I'm fine with them. My biggest thing is that I feel like I've lost so much time. So many of my memories are foggy," Lola says, glad Frog has finally arrived in her frontal lobe to be ready if needed but more glad that Stella hadn't elaborated on her voice message. *What could Frog have done? God, I hope they didn't start talking philosophy or politics. She knows I don't care about that stuff.*

"I do think you've made a lot of progress, Lola. I'm really proud of all the hard work you've done. I understand we've modified your medications, but normally they don't kick in quite this fast. You really owe yourself a pat on the back for all this progress," Dr. Hillcrest says. "I just have concerns about things staff have mentioned. Paul said you told him your name was Sam yesterday. That concerns me."

"It was a joke," Lola insists, glad at least Samantha had the foresight to warn her about that one. *Seven years old and smarter than the others.* "No one around here can take a joke. That's why I'm going to miss Clare so much."

"Do you think you'll have to lose Clare entirely though?" Dr. Hillcrest says, putting down his pen for the first time since the session began.

"Look, I have to be honest with you. I get the idea that when they—we—merge, no one loses anything and we all gain each other. I finally get to figure out who I truly am. They are only pieces of me and are all actually me. I do get that. But with them separate, the way it is now, the only way I

177

really know, I do feel like I have friends. Like people in my corner I can go to for different things. I go to Clare for laughs. I guess I just worry that I won't have that anymore. Where will I go when I want to laugh?" Lola asks. "It's like losing family or something, I don't know."

"I can understand why you would feel that way and it's not the first time I've heard this concern, Lola," Dr. Hillcrest says. "Are you having second thoughts about a merge?"

Lola wishes she was a better liar, but decides she's done enough lying and covering for one day. She's better off being honest. Recovery, after all, she reasons, doesn't have to look picture perfect. She nods and bows her head.

"I think it takes a certain bravery to admit that. I admire you, Lola," Dr. Hillcrest says, surprising her. "But maybe the way to think about this is that by merging, you are also setting them free. I mean, we all know Tim and Frog aren't exactly happy being the only guys in there. Maybe in a merge, they will be happier?"

Lola nods, shifting her weight to her left. "I hope so," she mumbles. "It's just a lot."

"It is a lot. And I'm hoping we can start seeing each other daily to work through it all. I have some news that I'm not sure you'll like, but I feel like it's important to be transparent with you," the doctor says.

Lola looks up.

"I'm retiring in three weeks and wanted to give you a heads up. Now, this may not impact you much, as I will be going part-time for a bit and slowly weaning myself out. Your work with Ann and the other therapists has been wonderful and you will have a great transition program and safety plan before anything changes," Dr. Hillcrest says. "I really do care about you and your recovery so I want to help you to make this as smooth as possible."

Lola feels like she's been punched in the stomach. But as the kick of Dr. Hillcrest words lands, she also feels relief. Maybe, with the doctor gone, she muses, it will be easier to fake a merge.

"How are you feeling?" Dr. Hillcrest asks.

"It's just a lot. And more. So a lot," Lola says, shrugging her shoulders and telling herself it's all going to work out. *Where is Maria?*

***

Rabbit

179

It cracks me up how Host always looks to Maria for help. I avoid Maria when I can. I like to figure out things for myself. If I have to ask someone for help, I ask Tim. He's logical and puts real thought into things. I wish Sam would see me like I see Tim. But Sam probably thinks her big sister—not even a decade older—can't know much more than she does. If I had to talk about my real feelings on the merge—not the script that Maria and Tim made us follow in the hypnosis thing—I'd say I'm pretty undecided. I understand why they all want out of this place. I really do. I want nothing more than to be able to be in the real world and make true friends my own age. But let's face it, not many teens are going to want to hang out with Host's body. Maybe Host could be a mentor?

Sometimes, I feel like a merge would be great. It would be like suicide without any pain or any of them yelling at me that it was my fault. I wouldn't have to feel like a murderer. When I think about suicide, I get jealous of halters. They have the ability to make that decision for themselves. I have to think about seven other people. It sucks.

Looking at Tina's arms made me want to cut. I miss the feeling of pain. I miss how it makes me feel alive—like a halter

180

instead of an alter. And when I get attention for it, I feel less lonely. I wish I could spend more time with Tina.

I'm worried that Zoe stole Tina's things. That will really piss me off. Sam's birthday is around the corner and if I could bet money, I'd bet Sam will get the Peter Pan DVD that's missing. I'd bet she'll get all the things that are missing. And maybe that's not so bad. I could get Tina's playlist. Then, I could bring it back. There's nothing wrong with borrowing, but I don't believe in stealing. It's probably why I can't steal Host's one and only life. I just don't see why we halters don't get lives of our own. Did I mention that no one even remembered my birthday this year? They always remembered, until Sam came along.

Frog and I have talked about this many times. His theory is that alters live inside Hosts to teach them and the alters around them lessons. That's very possible. Then, if we do it right, we get to come back in the next life reincarnated as halters ourselves. He says we all start off our next life where we ended in our last life, only a step up. I sort of like that theory. But, I do wonder sometimes, was my last life as a rabbit and his as an amphibian? Because if it's true, that really sucks. My bigger worry is what if his theory is reverse. What if we already were halters and are now working our way down to the Easter Bunny and Kermit the Frog? There's a good reason to merge—and kill ourselves—right there.

Chapter Fifteen:
Alternate Views

Lola and Dr. Hillcrest meet in a conference room the next day. At the end of a long table sits a laptop with a projector aimed at a blank white wall. Lola keeps her eyes on the table, not sure if she's ready to watch her alters in charge of her body.

"Are you ready?" Dr. Hillcrest asks.

Lola shrugs. "I guess I'm as ready as I'll ever be."

"I've cut out a lot of the small talk. What I'm really interested in you seeing is the highlights of the hypnosis sessions," Dr. Hillcrest says. "I think when you see that the alters really all are in favor of a merge, it may make you feel better about letting them go. I also think that in seeing how similar they are, you may realize that they really are all just parts of you. That's my intent, anyway."

Lola wishes he'd skip the prelude and get to the point. She nods, reminding herself the alters and she have a plan and part of it is to play the doctor's game.

"I'm going to do this in order. It's the same order I met with them, by age," he says. "If, at any time, you want me to stop

183

the tape or you experience any emotions that you feel are important to process, please let me know. It will be important that you stay in charge and don't let any of the others appear. This is for you and I only, do you understand, Lola?"

"Yes."

Dr. Hillcrest dims the lights and fidgets with the laptop until an image finally appears on the wall. It's surreal seeing herself sitting on the doctor's couch but having no memory of ever sitting with her hands folded in her lap like that. *Maria,* she reminds herself. *Makes sense.* It takes Dr. Hillcrest another minute or so to get the audio going. Lola's grateful for the time to watch Maria's gestures and body language – like a preview for what she's about to experience in watching an alter working as a host.

"...what you don't understand about Lola, Dr. Hillcrest, is that she's very accommodating. When she understands that we alters are ready for this, she will be more than happy to make the merge," Maria says.

Lola can't take her eyes off the scene playing out in front of her and searches her memory for any recall at all of this conversation. There's nothing.

"Do you think the others would agree with that assessment, Maria?" Dr. Hillcrest asks.

Maria nods Lola's head. *That's something I do a lot. We have that in common,* Lola tells herself. *Score one for Dr. Hillcrest there.*

"Let's face it. The one you will have the most trouble with will be Clare. But once she realizes a merge will mean we can get out into the real world and that maybe Lola will start a comedy tour or something— that her audience will be bigger in the real world—she might go along with it quite well," Maria says. "It's worth a shot, anyway."

Dr. Hillcrest pauses the video, then fast forwards to another scene marked by numbers in his notebook. "This is Tim— are you doing okay so far, Lola?"

Lola nods. *Don't nod. That's Maria's thing.*

Lola makes it through the rest of the videos without saying much. Her mind is racing too much to reach the alters or even hear what they have to say. She finds herself unusually annoyed with all of them, unable to determine if they are stealing her life or if she is stealing theirs. Either way, she feels mad. Red-faced and grateful for the dim lighting, she tries to take shallow breaths so Dr. Hillcrest won't notice.

***

"Did you tell her we were having a meeting? Why isn't she here?" Tim asks Maria. "She's the damned host here. We need her on board, Maria. I told you it wasn't a good idea to let her watch those videos alone."

"She wasn't alone. Me and Clare watched right along."

Maria cuts Zoe off and waves her hand at Tim. "She has a *right* to see those. She'll be here in a minute. Stay calm. You worry too much. Is everyone *else* here?" Maria quickly scans the frontal lobe and counts seven people. "Yes. Everyone's here. Sam, run and get Host."

"I'm coming!" Lola barks from a locked bathroom in the Rosewood hallway. "Give me a second. I have to be sure I'm alone. Do you really think me talking to myself right now is going to help any of us?"

"Sorry," Maria says, shocked at Host's tone. "Tim's getting antsy is all."

"Okay, I'm here. You can start," Lola says.

"Hey girl! I've missed you!" Clare shouts.

"Thanks."

"Did you hear about my stand up? It went awesome."

"Yes. Everyone's been talking about it. I don't know how you do it. Great job, Clare."

"Enough small talk, ladies. We need to do this fast. Host is right. She can't be seen talking to herself. What's on the agenda?" Tim asks.

"Who knows, who cares. What Zoe and I want to know is why we even have to fake a merge? Did you guys see how we rocked out those interviews with the halter doc? We were on fire!" Clare says. "I'm not merging no matter what ya'll say! I'm here to stay!"

Rabbit rolls her eyes.

The alters take turns arguing about whether to consider a merge, reconsider a merge, fake a merge, or all together keep things status quo and find another way out. Lola's mind drifts to Dr. Hillcrest's plan for discharge and termination. It's coming too soon, she concludes. *How am I ever going to fit into my family again with all these people in me? This is never going to work. Do they even care? Maybe I need to* make *them merge after all. I can't have two lives, two families. Or is it eight lives, two families?*

***

Samantha

Nobody ever asks me how I feel about stuff. "Just enjoy being a kid. It doesn't last forever, Samantha," they say. So it's because I'm a kid. I get that. They think I don't know stuff. They think they are protecting me but they aren't. They don't listen to what I feel. It's not fair. But I wouldn't trade being a kid for anything in the world. There's more good things about being a kid than bad things. I'm lucky because I have Zoe to look out for me, and Frog and Rabbit too. I also like doing things with Tim. That's why I don't want a merge. With a merge, everything would change and I'd lose my entire family. I don't know why Host doesn't understand that and it scares me. It even gives me nightmares. I don't want to talk about that anymore. Let's start over. Do over!

Since my birthday is coming up, I wonder if the first thing I can do is get rid of the 'antha' part of my name. It's so stupid, doesn't even belong there. It is just a ton of extra things, like legs on a snake.

I like snakes. I think that would be awesome if I could get a snake for my birthday, or maybe a pitbull. I don't want any of those stupid, ugly girly dogs that wear those dumb barrettes and things. Being eight is going to be so awesome. On my day I can do whatever I want! The other alters will have to do what I say because birthday means queen for a day. I won't wear a stupid dress though, they're so gross. You can't run in a dress, you can't do anything fun in a dress. Last year, Host let me be in charge all day to celebrate my birthday. Even Tim and Maria had to do what I said. It was awesome.

I also want a Peter Pan doll for my birthday. Peter Pan is so cool. I bet he can flip whatever rocks he wants and find all of the best stuff. I love Peter Pan. He never has to grow up. He can just have fun forever. That's what I want. I want to be able to hold a rock and fly. Just like Peter. I want to see what the world looks like from the clouds. And I never want to get older than ten.

You know what my favorite animal is? An eagle. They're so...big. I saw an eagle on TV once and it was just so massive. They're on the back of the quarter too. Did you know that? I wish I could be like...like a great big eagle. They fly everywhere and just have fun. And they scream real loud too. They go AHHHHHHH and everyone knows they are coming. Everyone knows when Peter Pan is coming too. I wonder if, for my birthday, I can be an eagle Peter Pan? Then I don't ever have to be anything else. I just don't want wings because then I can't lift the rocks.

If I could fly away on my birthday, after flipping over rocks and finding the really cool stuff, I want to go swimming. I like stuff in the ocean too but I've never been there. Only in my head. After I fly, I want to be a Shark Peter Pan because nobody wants to pick on a shark, or a shark Peter Pan. I would swim from one end of the ocean to the other until I see everything there is to see. I bet there is a ton to see too. Halters are good for one thing; they can draw some really great things in the books.

I want to see everything...but I don't want stuff to change either. That's bad. Halters always say things like that; 'the seasons change and everything changes and you grow up.' That's stupid. There's something Frog and Tim are right about. Being a girl stinks sometimes. You know what I really hate about other girls? Even Clare and Zoe? Why can't they do what boys do? I can. I can hit harder than any boy. I can run faster than any boy. I can play baseball, football, basketball, everything better than a boy. At least, I bet I can. Girls just wear stupid dresses and put on stupid make up and paint their stupid nails. Gross. Nail polish stinks and that gross lipstick never comes off. Stupid. But sometimes, when Tim and Frog won't play with me, I pretend I like those things. Because, like Rabbit says, sometimes it gets lonely in here.

Chapter Sixteen:
Merge?

Lola skips dinner to take some time for herself. The alters each had a day, she reasons, so she deserves one too. She reaches under her mattress for Stella's letters. Frantic, she quickly realizes she can't find the large manila envelope. She throws her mattress on the floor, running her hands over the box spring of her twin bed and spinning around the room, hoping it flew in a corner somewhere when she tossed the mattress. Instead, the only thing she can find is her journal, perched next to the mattress and spilling with loose papers.

She searches for nearly an hour—even through Tina's things—before realizing it's impossible for the letters to be in the tiny room. She runs into the bathroom to wash her face. Checking her watch, she realizes she only has an hour before Tina will return and take away the rare quiet time she has. She ignores Sam's request to play survival trivia. "Not now," she says out loud. "Go talk to the others. I need a nap."

Putting her bed back together, Lola considers where the letters could be. Half of the residents in this wing have had things go missing lately, she reminds herself, but nothing personal like letters. They were things like gadgets and stuffed animals. She searches her brain, avoiding the alters, to remember if anyone had personal letters, journals, or other items like them stolen. Nothing.

Sighing, she checks her watch and settles on her bed with her journal. She begins to write and the letters come out faster than her thoughts—almost. She writes:

Wednesday, April 23

Today was the worst day ever. Tina's blaming me for stealing her stupid music thing. I can't find Mom's letters anywhere. I miss Mom more than ever and I don't even know why. I'm tired of everyone. The alters are yelling at me about stupid things. They insisted they each got a day to be in charge and all they did is make trouble for me. Dr. Hillcrest is starting to make me think that a merge would be the best thing for all of us. I have a right to live my own life and the alters really are only parts of me. They can say I asked them to help me all day long but the truth is that I never asked anyone for any of this. Maria just showed up. I could have handled it myself. Every one of them just showed up. I didn't ask for help and lately, it all just feels like more trouble than it's worth.

I love them. All of them. Each for different reasons. But Dr. Hillcrest says I'm not doing them or me any favors by hanging on. He says they would be happier in a merge. They would have opportunities in a merge. Maybe I would do comedy if Clare was a bigger part of me. Maybe I would have kids if the Zoe in me had a chance to meet the love of my life. Obviously, my body is too old to have kids, but there's no reason I couldn't meet a man who already has kids and get to be a mother somehow. And Sam? She's never even lived outside of here. How is that fair? I feel like I'm keeping them trapped.

But they are trapping me too. They don't give me the time and space I need to be me. Look at what it takes just to get a few hours alone with my thoughts. I have to bark at a seven-year-old. And that doesn't feel good to either of us. That's not who I want to be. I feel like my every waking moment is up for vote. How should I spend it? What do we want to do? How can I please everyone? What should I eat that would make Clare and

Frog happy at the same time? How quickly can I pee so that Tim doesn't have to think about the fact that I'm sitting, not standing? It's just too much.

I'm supposed to go through those letters. I'm supposed to use the past and the present and the memories I have to patch together who I am. I can't do that without the letters. And I can't let Dr. Hillcrest in on it that I don't have them. All these years, Maria's dealt with Mom. I know she's hiding something but it's not worth a fight to find out what. I'm not sure I even want to know. I know Maria has good intentions and if she thinks I shouldn't know it's for a good reason. I just have no clue how I'm supposed to figure out who I am when I have about an eighth of the memories I should have and now don't even have those letters to patch things together. Where could they have gone? I feel so crazy.

I'm tired of feeling crazy. I want to be one person who doesn't have voices inside of me. Maybe that's who I am. Maybe I'm strong and maybe I want to be strong for the first time in my life. Ann or one of the other therapists told me that it takes strength and resilience to even know how to create alters to protect yourself. Maybe it's time I stop relying on

195

the alters and instead rely on myself. If the strength's in there, maybe it's time I stepped up and used it. Then, when they ask me who I am, I could at least say, "I'm Lola and I'm strong."

I want my old life back. The life that made sense. I want to get to know Charlotte again. I barely got time with her before I started going crazy. I want to meet her kids and spend time with my real family. Is that so wrong? Doesn't everyone have a right to understand who they are, where they come from, and be around the people who have stood by them? But where would that leave the alters? They have stood by me. And they are my family! In a merge, would they be loved and embraced by my family too? Would it mean we could all finally be a family? Maybe that's it. Maybe that's the point. And maybe, it's time for me to put my foot down and insist we at least try. Because nothing else is working.
–Lola, Large and in Charge (Great, now I sound like Clare)

***

Tim

LOLA, PARTY OF EIGHT   ERIN LEE

If Host could go back on faking a merge—or worse, try to force a legit merge—we need a back-up plan. It's definitely about time that I get the chance to do what needs to be done. No one else is going to do anything to get it done. It's always up to me in the end. "Tim will fix it. Ask Tim," they say. The girls? Time for them to sit this one out. Frog can keep an eye on them. This is going to work. I have spent way too much time coming up with plans to get the hell out of this place and nobody, and I mean nobody is going to get in the way. But this here? This is the best one yet.

For one, we need a distraction. At first I thought a fight would be the best thing, but that isn't a big enough scale—no, it has to be bigger. A fire alarm is definitely the way to go. A fire alarm isn't enough though, not at all. We need an actual fire to burn because if there isn't any smoke then there isn't any evacuation, there aren't any halter fire fighters, EMTs, and there aren't any halter cops and you need those things. A little bit of camouflage will go a long way, that's for damn sure.

As far as how I'm going to get fire? Well, that's as easy as 1-2-3; I'm in a woman's body. Host may pride herself as being a feminist, but she still has tits and

197

those can be used better than any other weapon of deception. Learn your enemies and their weakness and exploit them. I can smell the cigarettes on some of those halter orderlies and some of them are young and dumb. I keep my eyes on them constantly because I'm ready for them if they put their hands on her. I have no issue breaking bones for protection, but I think that seduction can work too; easier for this. Yeah, it will be disgusting as all get out to let those pukes put hands on Host, but sometimes you have to make some sacrifices for the greater good.

I think the new halter—Brown—will be the target of choice. He's about twenty years old and just has the look of a wannabe player. He's about six one, looks like he lives in the gym, has the stupid tattoos on his arm that he thinks makes him look cool, and the pencil thin moustache. Just a joke, really. He thinks he's God's gift, but he can be controlled with no problem. I've gotta get in Host. Will promise him some…'fun' if he can get me some outlawed item or other. When I get what I want, it should be just after lunch if I plan it out right, and tell him before his shift ends at eight he will get a thank you.

The fire will come at about three or so. Halter cops work ten hour shifts so around three in the afternoon the morning shift cops will be ready to wind down for the next shift. If I'm lucky, the halter firefighters and EMTs will be exhausted since they are usually working twenty-four or forty-eight hour shifts at a time. I will have to do more research on that.

The fire will be in the janitor's closet as well. Even though the stuff in there is to keep the other nut jobs from trying to kill themselves, some of that stuff can still be flammable. Plus some clothing will help out as an accelerant. Make a good healthy fire in the janitor's closet, slip out, and then wait. When the fire alarm sounds they will have to get us off of the unit. When they get us out it will be pandemonium because as much as they try to keep the other halters under control, they will be so excited about what's going on that they won't be orderly and that's when we slip away.

Depending on who we run into first; halter security guards, police, fire fighters, EMTs…it doesn't really matter one way or the other. The plan will be the same. We jump them, switch clothes, and we get the hell out of here. It's as simple as that. While it's probably easier said than done, and there will be need for improvisation somewhere along the line, all we are going to need is a distraction and that won't be any problem.

I will probably have to make some good use of some physical geometry and some wit, but that won't be too hard. So long as Host and the girls just stay the hell out of my way and Frog keeps them distracted and lets me work, we'll be out of here. I'm sick of sitting, waiting, being silenced, and being trapped in this Godforsaken scumhole. I will not be locked up any longer, that's for damn sure. All it takes is taking advantage of some weak-willed halter having his brains used against him. By the end of this week we'll be out of here and it will be all because of me. It will be about time that I'm given the credit I deserve. Unless, of course, the girls can stick to the plan today and I can avoid this whole thing all together. Shit, the meeting. Gotta run. Keep your fingers crossed I don't have to resort to this. But I will.

***

"Guys, it's not time to joke around. She's seriously going to try to merge us for darn sure. The only way out of this is we have to find a way to be quiet and let her think we've merged. Let her and the doctors think the meds have done it," Tim says. "I've run every other possible scenario and this is the only one that will work."

"Ya'll, I think he's right. I'm not letting her absorb us into some blob of a personality. Because let's face it, with Tim and Maria in there with us, we won't be able to have any fun at all," Clare says.

The other alters, except Maria, nod in agreement. Maria objects with, "I don't think I ruin all your fun. I just try to keep everyone safe. You guys have to think about Host too. How is she going to get along without us? And do you really think we can trick her? How are we going to stay quiet for that long? We're at Rosewood for at least three more weeks. The halters will find out that—"

"No. Not this time. The only one who might be a problem is Sam. But we can keep her busy. Zoe can take her down to the basement—feet—and have movie marathons, *Peter Pan*. We need to tell her it will mean a trip to Disneyland or something. Give her a reason to want to work with us. Look, Maria, we even have Clare on board," Tim says. "Don't make me resort to plan B. It's messy."

"You really think we're going to be able to get a seven-year-old to stay quiet for that long?" Maria asks. "And knock it off with your stupid plans."

"Eight. She'll be eight by that time," Zoe says before being shushed by Tim's glare.

"I see no reason this can't work," Frog says. "Tim's right. If Rabbit and I can keep Sam distracted and get her to understand that we only have to stay quiet for a month or so, those stupid halters will let Host go. No one says we have to be quiet after that. We can tell her it will be like taking a long nap or something. What do you think, Zoe?"

Zoe jumps right in. "I don't even think we can show up right away. I think we have to go missing, totally disappear, for like six months. And that means Sam's birthday. Which is horrible. But they aren't going to let Host go without supervision. That whole transition thing. I think we have to find a way to stay quiet for six months or even more. It's going to be hard but will be so worth it. We could get on a seven day schedule. We could each get one day of the week or something. We could finally be free and live real lives. I don't know any other choice. Host is getting scared. She's being brainwashed by that doctor. We need to do something now. It's either that or go back to Tim's plan of an actually escape. But then where will we be? It's not like Host knows how to survive. And we won't be able to stay at her mother's."

The six oldest alters weigh the pros and cons of faking a merge for several hours before finally deciding to take a vote. In the end, it's unanimous, except for Sam, who they decide is too young to vote anyway.

"We begin today. Right away," Tim declares. "It's settled."

"But what about goodbye? Host is going to freak out and be—"

"That's *exactly* why there *can't* be a goodbye."

***

Maria, have you seen my shampoo?
Silence.
Maria?
Silence.
Maria? Where the heck is everyone? It's never this quiet.

Lola had slept better than she had in years last night and felt better about the alters after venting in her journal and a good night's sleep. But now, with dripping hair and no shampoo, she wants her normal life back. That life includes Maria always knowing where she's misplaced things and being around to help, including in the shower.

She grabs her towel from the hook on the outside of the modest shower stall. Her flip-flops flap as she walks in circles around the tiny shared bathroom, trying to spot where Tina moved the shampoo. *Great. I guess I don't get to wash my hair today. Maria? Where are you?*

Lola closes her eyes as she dresses. The room is unusually quiet, with Tina already off to breakfast and the hallways basically empty. *Maria? Are you okay? I'm late today because you didn't wake me up. Frog? Where's Maria? It's breakfast time. Sam? You must be here. You wouldn't leave. Sam?*

Silence.

Lola looks around the empty room and under the closed door for signs of anyone walking by – there are none. "Guys! Wake up! We're late. Breakfast started a half hour ago. And has anyone seen my shampoo?"

But no one answers. And it stays that way all day, and the next, and the next, and the next. Lola has never been so grateful for her one monthly individual session with group therapist Ann. She needs someone to talk to.

"The voices are just, well, gone. I have tried everything to get them to talk to me," she confesses.

"But I don't understand," Ann says, scribbling in her notebook. "Isn't this a good thing? Weren't you and Dr. Hillcrest working toward getting them to merge? Wasn't that the *point* of the new medications? The dosage change?" Ann flips through a thick file. Lola wishes she would stop playing catch-up and look up from her paperwork.

"Yes. That was the plan. That is the plan. That's what it takes to get discharged. But I guess I thought I would have a chance to say goodbye or something. I was pretty mad at them but it was only for a day or two. I've been mad at them before and they never just…disappeared…like this," she says. "I'm not even mad anymore, I just miss them."

Ann finally looks up. "This is good stuff, Lola. You have made *such* progress. I know you don't see it now, but it is. I can understand how this would be scary for you. You are going to need to grieve this. Who are your supports? You haven't told the group about this yet. Maybe they could be helpful?"

Sure, a group of other crazy people whose primary concern will be who is going to make them laugh now that Clare's MIA. "I'm not ready to tell anyone. I'm not ready for them to be gone." Lola wants to cry but holds back. *You need to stay strong. You need to find a way to do this alone. This is what you wanted. Maybe you're really cured. Maybe you can do this on your own. Give it a chance.*

"What about your mother, or your step-sister, or someone?" Ann persists.

"I haven't talked to my step-sister, Charlotte, in years. I can barely remember the last time. And Mom is already terrified I'm going to flake out and kill myself or end up right back in here after I go home. I don't really need to worry them with my mourning—grieving as you said—the loss of my 'imaginary friends,' do you think?

"I think it might be good to give them a chance. Your discharge is so close and you're going to need people on the outside who understand your illness and can support you. And there's always the possibility that the alters are just taking a break—on vacation for a bit, shall we say.

Have you considered how you would handle it if they came back?"

"You aren't listening. I would *like* them to come back at this point. It's scary being alone in my head. It's how I got here in the first place, I'd assume," Lola says, cracking her knuckles. *Frog cracks his knuckles. Have we already merged?*

"These are all things you can go over with Dr. Hillcrest in the next few weeks. But I need to warn you, he's going to see this as a great thing too. We all are. It's healthiest for you to be fully merged. It's only after a merge that the true work of recovery can really begin."

Great. That's six more sessions I get to fake that I'm okay if I'm ever going to get out of here. I can't stay in here without the alters. At least by going home, I'll have Mom and Charlotte and Travis. Fake it 'til I make it, that's what I'll do. That's what Zoe would say.

***

"I'm bored, though! And this is lame down here. I don't understand why we can't go upstairs and watch TV from the couch like normal people, Zoe," Sam whines. "We've been down here for like forever and I'm sick of whispering! And

207

what day is this? Isn't my birthday coming soon?"

"I know it's hard, Sam," Zoe whispers. "But you need to be good. You want to go to Disney, right? Just a quick trip? Just the eight of us? We can't do that if Host is stuck in the hospital. We need you to be really grown up."

"But I don't want to grow up! Peter Pan wouldn't grow up! Eight is okay, but nothing past ten," Sam says. "And I'm sick of TV. I want to run around and play games. And I miss Host. We never see her anymore. Are we mad at her?"

"No! We aren't mad at all. We're helping her. We need to be quiet so she can concentrate. Remember, you need to whisper."

Sam lowers her voice and says, "Rabbit doesn't think this is a good idea. Rabbit wants to do what the halters want, I heard her tell that to Frog. Why doesn't Rabbit think this is a good idea?"

Zoe looks at Sam and wishes she— herself—could be so innocent. "Rabbit's confused. You know how she is. Rabbit's never happy. You, on the other hand, are like me. We make the best of things. Now, come on, I need you to be really good. It won't be much longer. Can you do that for me? For us?"

Sam crosses her arms over her chest and nods. "I guess. But I miss Tim and Frog. Why can't they be down here too? I hate them being in the attic so far away and all quiet and stuff. This sucks."

Zoe doesn't bother to correct Sam's language. *It sure does.* "Why don't you let me do your nails for you? Wouldn't that be fun? Or we could play with your birthday presents again?"

"Gross. Never mind. Let's watch *Peter Pan*. If I do ever grow up. If I like, have to, I'm gonna marry Peter Pan."

Chapter Seventeen:
Homecoming

On May 12, discharge eve, Dr. Hillcrest wastes no time asking Lola how she feels about termination.

I feel like I'm making the biggest move of my life without the only people who truly understand me. I don't exactly feel great. While she knew this was coming, Lola is surprised at how relaxed he is about it. She asks herself, *What did you expect? He has to act okay with this. He's believing in you* for *you. Besides, he's retiring anyway. What does he care?*

"...and that meets three days a week. It's over at the main hospital. The discharge coordinator will show you where. It's important that you go to all of these, Lola. You'll recognize many of the faces. It's mostly the same group you already attend now on Mondays, Wednesdays and Fridays. A few changes, but not many. Mary, the resources director, is making up a list of all of this and your mother will have one too, to help you remember," Dr. Hillcrest says. "Are you following me?"

210

Lola nods, wishing Maria was around to write this all down. *Why didn't she say goodbye?*

"Okay. I promise this isn't going to be as scary as it seems. There will be ups and downs, of course, but we are right here and I'm only a phone call away," he says. "You can do this, Lola. I know you can."

"Thanks," Lola says, desperate to believe him. "Are you sure I shouldn't be going into a halfway house or something? I mean, I know you said the transition would need to be slow. I'm just not sure I'm ready to…"

Dr. Hillcrest looks Lola in the eye. "I wouldn't sign off on this if I didn't think you were ready, Lola. It will be important for you to have support around. There will be no better support than your family. I was so pleased to learn your mother was willing to let you stay with her. You'll be just fine. If you have any sign that the alters are coming back I want you to call me immediately. Don't freak out. We may just need to tweak your meds," Dr. Hillcrest says. "Promise?"

"I promise. Thanks," Lola says. "Thanks for everything."

* * *

Lola leaves Dr. Hillcrest's office with mixed emotions. While her time with him has been helpful and she knows she's made great progress, she can't help but feel abandoned by yet another person. *You're being ridiculous,* she tells herself. *No one has abandoned you. You* made *them leave. You wanted your own life back! You basically willed them away. You know they can read. They probably read every word of your journal. You asked for this.*

She doesn't speak to Paul as she follows him down the corridor back to the inpatient wing of the hospital. Instead of racing to the Internet or dayroom as she usually does, Lola goes to her room to think. She almost stops herself, remembering the last time she took time for thinking and how it had made the alters disappear. But there is so much to think about and she feels like she might finally have some answers: *The key is to be your own best friend now. Accept yourself the way you accepted your alters. Stop hiding behind them and live your life, Lola. It's time. This is why they left. They left because they knew you needed them to. Not because they abandoned you.*

Lola spends her last dinner at Rosewood with that same spirit. Instead of allowing Edna's anxiety to irritate her, she spends extra time helping the woman feel safe. She offers Justin her fruit cup before he asks for it. She makes a special effort to listen to Tina's latest suicide plan without judgment or trying to intervene. She understands the importance of feeling heard without judgment. And she keeps her mouth shut as Lindsay rattles on with a list of every drug she's ever tried and every man who's ever "serviced" her in her youth. Like it or not, she realizes, these real-life patients are no different or more guilty than the ones she'd created in her head.

Paul stops by the table and produces a handmade card from under his clipboard.

"We all made this for you to wish you luck and congratulate you for getting out," he says, motioning toward Lola's group of friends.

Lola is touched as Justin stops eating for a moment to watch her open the card.

"We wanted to go to the card store and get you a gift too," Lindsay says. "But you know how cheap these people are. 'Too much gas,' they said. 'Not till the weekend.'" Lindsay crinkles her nose and shoots a dirty look at the nearest staffer.

Tina agrees.

"God forbid we get out of here for two seconds. Whatever happened to field trips?" she asks.

Lola laughs and opened the card.

"No. This is perfect," she says. "Thank you."

Everyone she knows at Rosewood has taken the time to sign and some even draw pictures. The first note to get her attention is from Paul:

Dear Lola,

For three years I watched you stare out a window. I would go in your room and talk to you about my silly problems. It was nice having someone—any of you—to listen to me. Even though you didn't always hear me, it was so nice having someone there to bounce things off of. And, it was interesting to be able to get different perspectives. I don't think you will ever know the impact that you have had on my life without even knowing it.

I'm thrilled that you are finally back and I know you will be successful. I believe in you, Lola.

Best wishes,

Paul

Lola fights the mist creeping into her eyes. She continues reading:

Dear Lola,

214

Our time together has come to an end. But I'm never more than a phone call away. And I'm not just saying that.

I hope you are as impressed as I am with how far you have come and how quickly. You owe yourself some pretty heavy credit for the work you've done.

Thank you for allowing me into your world and for trusting me. I know how difficult that can be.

Remember, I'm a control freak—as you and Clare have so often rightly reminded me—and would never set you up to fail. I know you can do this. Don't go back inside. The world needs you on the outside.

All the best,
Dr. Ted

And,

Hey Lola,

You're finally getting out. Rock on! Load up on some good net time and music. God knows I wish I could. Thanks for always knowing where my shit was. You were a good roommate. See you on the other side.

Tina

And,

Dear Lola,

Thanks for all your dinners. I'll miss you.

Justin

And,

You are okay. You're not gonna die.
Love, Edna

And,

Lola,

I didn't know you long but you were
always nice to me. Make sure to go out
and buy yourself a reward for getting out
of here. I usually go to the Ingenuity
Store on Main Street. I'll call you when
I'm out. We can shop together. You can
never have enough crazy friends.

Love,

Lindsay

PS—Find a man. A girl needs to get
laid every now and then. It helps the
crazy.

Lola laughs, wipes her tears, and thanks
the group again.

"I'll miss you guys too. Thank you,"
she says.

***

Later, one of the first things Lola
notices as she exits the front doors of
Rosewood is the patient registration sign.
She recognizes it as the one she could see
out of her grimy window for so many
years before being transferred into the

room with Tina. She inhales the fresh spring air and closes her eyes, standing still for a moment before following Stella to her car.

Don't think about it. Don't think about them. This is your life. Now you need to live it. A new beginning for you and for you alone. You're in charge and you can do this.

Lola rides in the back of Stella's Subaru—she hasn't ridden in the front of any vehicle since her accident as a teen and Stella isn't pushing it today—as her mother babbles about what's for dinner and asks her at least thirty times how great it is that she's finally coming home. Travis, who'd offered her the front seat, is quiet but often looks back at Lola as if worried she'll jump out of the car. *We should all be so lucky.*

***

Lola's nostrils recoil at the familiar scent of patchouli in her mother's house as she steps in the front door. Being in Stella's home gives Lola her first detailed childhood memory; something she isn't sure she's prepared for: playing Barbie dolls with Holly in the foyer. *Holly. Is. Dead. It's. Your. Fault.* She wishes Maria was here and quickly puts the memory out of her mind. *Besides,* she thinks, *Maria would find reasons to pick on Mom.* She never understood why Maria was so against Stella—*jealousy, maybe?* She puts her bag on her mother's couch and asks Stella to get her a tea so she can have a private moment to take it all in. Fortunately, Stella agrees.

With her mother gone, Lola considers what going into her room will be like. Will it look the same? Will the Def Leppard posters still be there? Hadn't her mother said she'd made some changes? *God, I hope so.* She's happily surprised to find a tastefully decorated bedroom; complete with lavender curtains and creamy walls. It's nothing like the childhood bedroom she'd left behind. Instead, it reminds her of something out of a popular home design magazine Zoe often read and collected at Rosewood. *What was that name of that magazine?*

"Is it okay?" Stella asks, surprising Lola from the doorway. "We saved your old stuff. It's in the attic. We made sure nothing was thrown out but we thought you could use a change."

"Mom, It's perfect," she says. "Thank you."

"Oh! I'm *so* relieved!" Stella says. "It's hard to know what you like now, after all these *years*."

"Thanks."

"Well, your tea's downstairs but steaming hot. Why don't you get settled for a few minutes and then come down? I want to make a nice dinner for us tonight. Just you and Travis and I. We thought the quiet time getting used to things might be the best thing for you tonight until you're used to being home again. This weekend we'll get everyone together. They all miss you too. And I'm excited for you to meet the kids."

Lola exhales. "That sounds great, Mom. I'll grab that tea in a few minutes. Then, I think I'm going to take a bath and then a nap and see how I feel when I get up," Lola says. "It's been so long since I've had a tub."

"Spoken just like my old Lola. I put new bubble bath in the bathroom for you. I'll be downstairs if you need anything," Stella says. "And Dragonfly? I'm glad you're home. I've waited a long time for this."

"I'm glad to be home, Mom," Lola says, smiling big enough to cause her shy dimples to appear.

***

The general volume at Stella's house on family dinner night Saturday hurts Lola's ears. She'd worked so long and hard to finally hear silence in her head. But she doesn't want to complain. She understands that the noise is just a reflection of the excitement the people who love her most have at her being back in their lives. She reminds herself to be patient as her family members shout over one another and made overly conscientious efforts to include her in every conversation. She finds it comical that a psychiatric hospital was quieter than her childhood home is now.

This is enough to make anyone nuts. Who could blame me?

Lola's nine-year-old niece, Aubree, hasn't stopped talking to her since she walked in the door. She tells her aunt all about life in the third grade, which boys she likes, which boys she doesn't like, her favorite subjects, and so on. Her brother Will isn't far behind her. For him, the stories are about kindergarten and which dinosaur was the biggest. The young boy is a wealth of knowledge about dinosaurs and reptiles. Lola misses Sam.

"Who wants to sit next to Aunt Lola?" Stella sings from the kitchen.

The house smells of coconuts and lemon as Stella puts the finishing touches on her lemon chicken recipe and the kids shout "me!" in unison. Lola still can't get over the idea of her own mother being a grandmother and how well she is doing, considering her age.

"You're in luck!" Lola says, pretending she's talking to Sam and Rabbit. If there's one thing she's good at, it's multi-tasking other people's needs. "There are two sides of me. One can sit on the left, one on the right!"

"I know my left and right! I learned it in school. Do you know your left and right, Aunt Lola?"

It's startling to hear the wide-eyed little boy call her "aunt." Her mother had said her step-sister Charlotte had kept her memory alive, but Lola hadn't known to what degree until meeting the children herself.

"Of course I do!" She laughs, feeling good to be part of a family. Oddly, though, she misses Justin's pleads for the extra food on her tray as everyone eats off their own plates and dinner conversation turns to real world small talk. She also misses plastic silverware, which makes her miss Zoe. *It's okay. It's just going to take time. Go with it.*

"How does being home make you feel now that you've had a few days, Lola?" Charlotte asks. "Is Mom driving you nuts yet?"

"Oh, Charlotte! L-leave your sister alone! I have been nothing but helpful. H-haven't I, Lola?" Stella stammers. Lola can't help but feel a bit jealous of her mother and step-sister's clearly close relationship.

"It's been good, Charlotte. Don't worry about me. I'm still settling in. I'm going to look into signing up for some classes and getting a job soon enough. First, though, I have to figure out how to get my license back," Lola says. She doesn't want to think about the last time she drove.

"Do you need to take a road test again?" Travis asks. "I'd be happy to practice with you."

"Thanks," Lola says. "I think I have to start all over but I'm not sure."

"My Lola was always a great driver, a natural. It's really too bad we never got you your lic—" Stella says, looking from Lola to her dinner plate. She quickly adds, "Charlotte, on the other hand..."

Lola puts down her fork.

Charlotte smacks her husband, Will, before he can laugh at his step-mother-in-law's comment.

"Shut up!" she scolds her husband, gently smacking his chest. "We don't need comments from the peanut gallery. And no one asked you anyway, brat! Geesh. A couple of minor fender benders and you would think you'd killed somebody!" No sooner are the words out before the room goes silent.

Lola turns red. *Don't think about it. Say something. They are all uncomfortable. Fix it. Maria would know what to do. No! You don't need Maria!* "Can someone pass the salt?"

Later, Lola wants to be annoyed with the niece she's never known, her mother, all of them...except for Charlotte. However, she can't help how warm she feels. Everyone is more careful to avoid another collision with topics like Holly and Stella's focus becomes quality family time and random chatter; something Aubree has no problem helping facilitate.

"Aunt Lola, do you think that if I keep my curls just like yours Alexander will like me? Daddy says I'm too young to go out on dates. What do you think Aunt Lola? Aunt Lola, do you—..."

"Now Aubree, your aunt doesn't need to have you throwing questions at her like this is Twenty Questions, all right?" Will says kindly, yet firmly. His New England accent takes a sharpness that is slightly more menacing than he intends it to come across. His electric blue eyes have strength that Lola can tell is not used to being disobeyed. He looks like a working class, modern day version of Rhett Butler with his blue jeans, white t-Shirt and brown boots.

"Yes, Daddy," Aubree replies, looking down; her eyes starting to well with tears.

"I'm sorry for her. She can be very...enthusiastic. Especially when it comes to you. You know Charlotte wouldn't let you be a stranger to the kids." Will smiles.

"It's all right, Will, thank you. I'm just really tired," Lola begins.

"And I bet, you're overwhelmed. I get it." Will says. "Oh dang it! William Junior! You know better than to get into your paint in the living room!"

Will is up in a flash to reprimand his son, who is his physical miniature.

"God, I just wish that I could go upstairs and..." Lola mutters to herself as her mother bursts into the living room.

Charlotte looks at her stepsister sympathetically.

"I have coconut cake for dessert! How about a game?" Stella calls cheerfully.

"Um, Dear?" Travis asks cautiously. "I think Lola is a little tired. It's already eight. Maybe we should—"

"Nonsense!" Stella retorts. "This is our first time as a *full* family and we are going to *enjoy* it! We have cake, we have family, and now we'll have games! What should we play?"

"Candyland! " Will yells from the corner as he helps his father clean up his mess.

"I don't want to play Candyland! I hate Candyland! It's stupid!" Aubree screams.

"It is not stupid!" Will yells back.

"Yes it is!" Aubree snaps. "It's for babies!"

"No it—"

"Aubree, that's *enough*," Charlotte snaps.

She's tired too. If only she could understand that this is what it's sounded like in my head all these years, Lola thinks.

"Oh now, you two!" Stella chuckles as she sets the cake down on the coffee table. "That's quite enough of that! Your Aunt Lola is home and we are going to be nice! We don't want her to think we're a family of wild turkeys or anything now, do we?"

"No Grandma." The siblings reply in unenthusiastic unison.

Grandma. Jesus, that sounds weird.

"Good. Because Grandma doesn't believe in all of that hissy fit nonsense. Now, I was thinking maybe we could play, how about Uno?" Stella suggests.

Lola sighs lightly. "Mom, I'm kind of tired and—"

"Oh only a few hands, it'll be fine, believe me." Stella smiles.

Oh. My. Gawwwwd. This woman still can't take a hint! How am I going to live here? Maria's right. She's impossible.

"Honey, maybe we should just call it a night?" Travis suggests.

Brave guy. Crazy even. Nobody tells Stella 'no' when she has her mind set on something.

"Oh Travis, don't be an old man! Just a few hands, all right?" Stella insists.

Travis rolls his eyes and sits down in his easy chair, knowing that Stella is pushing and isn't going to be reeled in by anyone.

"Come on, sweetie," Travis said to Aubree. "Come sit with Grampy."

Aubree curls up in Travis's lap as Stella deals out the cards.

Lola looks at Charlotte, who returns her sister's reproachful glance.

Stella deals the cards, oblivious to the fact that she's pretty much the only person in the room interested in playing. She smiles wider and hums as she looks at her cards.

Great poker face, Ma. "Oh, God." Lola groans.

"Yeah, I know." Charlotte laughs.

"She's about to win big." Will laughs as he looks to his hand. "Why do you always deal me piss poor hands, Stella?"

"Because, my sweet son-in-law, I may be big on family time, but I *really* love to *win*!" Stella snickers, high-fiving Aubree.

Lola can't help but shake her head as her persistent mother's personality lifts the somber mood that had attempted to overtake them. As she organizes her own cards, she looks over to Charlotte, who hisses, "Stop looking at my cards, you cheater!"

"I am not looking at your stupid cards!" Lola retorts.

"Lola!" Charlotte growls.

"Charlotte!" Lola growls.

"Girls! Come on and throw in so I can win this hand, please? You sound like a couple of wet hens fighting over a rooster!" Stella perks an eyebrow.

"Daddy!" Will groans. "I don't like blue cards, I want red ones!"

"Well, son, we don't have any yet," Will says.

"Well, I want some," Will says, reaching for the deck.

"No, sweetie! You can't take those cards yet. Here, how about Grandma will give you a few of her cards and she'll just grab a few more." She hands over some of her red cards and takes a few from the deck as Will pays more attention to the cards than to the game itself.

"And Uno!" Stella calls.

"Mom! I swear all you do is cheat at Uno!" Lola groans.

"It's not cheating when you're just great, my dear," Stella taunts. "Besides, I was just helping my grandson."

For the next three hours, Lola forgets about her headache and her journal. Her mother's jovial laughter, her playful banter with her step-sister, and even enjoying her rambunctious niece and nephew, make her feel safe for the first time since she can remember.

Soon, the cake is gone and the two children are sleeping soundly on the floor. Will stands with a groan.

"All right, we need to get going, Stella. If we were playing for money you'd have the mortgage on the house. As it stands, I have to head to work in the morning and the kids have church."

"Yeah, I have to head in tomorrow for a few hours too." Travis yawns. "I hate working on weekends. How many times have I retired now? I never learn."

"Oh, you two poops! You're just mad because you can't handle being beaten," Stella says. "Men!"

Charlotte and Lola hug close with their goodbyes, promising to call each other tomorrow and to get together soon.

Charlotte's family isn't gone thirty seconds before Stella starts with her questions. "So did you have a good time, sweetheart?" Stella asks as she collects the plates for the sink.

"I did, Mom. Thank you. I didn't really—"

"You didn't want all of this because you just wanted to sit in that cave of a room of yours and brood while you scribbled in your journal," Stella finishes for her with a grin. "Remember something, young lady, I know you. And I know that you needed this tonight. That's why I pushed for it. You needed to be around your family. I *never* gave up on you, Dragonfly. Not *ever*. And to have you here, the entire family together…well, this wasn't just for *you*. It was for *me* too." Stella can't hide the tears in her eyes.

"Mom…" Lola begins.

"Don't you dare. You went through so much but you're better now and that's all that matters. You're better, you're home, and our family is together again," Stella proclaims.

I wish it was going to be that easy. "Yeah. Yeah, I am. Thanks for tonight, Mom. I think I'm going to go to bed," Lola says, feeling sixteen again. "Good night."

"Good night, Dragonfly."

Chapter Eighteen:
Taking Charge

By September, Lola has been successful at meeting many of her goals. For starters, she's earned her driver's license. It feels good to drive again, this time with a license, and Stella loaned her the money to buy a car. She'd purposely stayed away from a Subaru—the car she once drove in her mind when Maria was in charge and the one she'd seen her mother drive away from Rosewood so many times without even realizing it. Instead, she opted for a white Jeep Wrangler with black interior. Her vanity plate reads LOLA1. Her only regret is that she can't show it to Clare, who she knows would have loved riding in it with the top down.

Lola has also reconnected with old friends. She's amazed at how quickly social networking sites aided in that endeavor—*no wonder there was such a fuss about the Internet*. From high school friends who never even knew she went missing to a new friendship with Lindsay, who's just been released from Rosewood herself, Lola keeps herself busy during her free time. Though it's sometimes easier to stay in the safety of Stella's familiar home, she knows getting out is important to her ongoing recovery.

She hasn't missed a therapy session since her release from Rosewood nearly four months ago. She's often the first one at group sessions and the last to leave. She no longer cares about where she sits and speaks her mind in group therapy instead of saying what she thinks the therapist wants to hear—like many of her sessions for years at Rosewood. And best of all, she speaks long term for herself, and only herself.

So far, none of the alters have returned. Lola believes she's making a conscious choice every day not to go back inside herself. However, she knows that it might not be that easy. She constantly reminds herself of the importance of taking her medication and isn't so cocky to think she is cured.

This week, she plans to write a letter to her biological father. She hopes to be able to forgive him for abandoning her, no matter how Stella wants to describe it. She realizes—from all her therapy work—relationships work two ways and she only has her mother's side of the story. While she will never forget what her father did, she also knows it's important to her own healing to reach out to him; an idea Stella isn't particularly fond of.

A determined Lola inhales the crisp air as she walks to her mother's mailbox. She's thrilled to see her first set of books for her basic psychology class have arrived. The class will be a breeze with everything she's seen. She's anxious to put all the new information she's learned about herself and so many others to use. For months she's been researching mental illness and attending multiple group and individual sessions. Soon, she'll even open up to them about how much she misses her alters; make them finally understand that they never were imaginary. She's even managed to get Stella, Travis, and Charlotte into a support group so they can better understand and support her. She's trying to do all the right things. *Maria would be so proud. And Clare would die to know I've joined a gym.*

She has a routine of taking her medications daily. She knows full well what will happen if she stops her meds. While they sometimes leave her feeling groggy, they keep her two lives separate; something she desperately needs if she's going to catch up on the business of living a real life. She recently watched a documentary about a man from Oregon who refused treatment and thought nothing was wrong with him. While she can understand how he felt, she also watched his decline after deciding not to take his medications. She doesn't want that for herself. At the same time, she can't help but feel guilty about abandoning the alters. She can't quite decide if they are a part of her now or if they have just evaporated all together.

There's a certain pride she feels in finally accepting that she has a mental illness. She now views herself as resilient. The world she created points to her creativity and an imagination as vivid as any artists. She'd managed to keep a world which had brutalized her at bay while she healed and created a new one. She'd constructed a world where she has control over people's pain—including her own. She's proud of herself.

She's even managed to become grateful to the staff at Rosewood. She knows things could have been a lot harder at the hospital and that she's lucky not to have been locked away in an insane asylum forever; as they'd done in the 40s and 50s. Lola knows that half of the country's mass killings in the past 50 years—most of which she'd missed during her time inside herself—were committed by people with mental illness; specifically schizophrenia. She can't imagine intentionally hurting anyone, ever. But more importantly, Lola's research on identity disorders tells her she isn't alone. Millions of Americans are just like her and struggle with their illness every day. *We're all a little crazy. Just in different ways.*

***

Lola thinks about Edna as she drives her new Jeep to the community college to register for one additional class. She realizes it was just the old woman's spirit coming through when she spouted off. It was as if her 'crazy' was talking and saying "I'm still here!" before retreating back into the silence Lola now understands so well.

We're all the same. And we're all going to be okay.

"But not *me*! *I'm* not going to be okay! It's boring as hell in here, ya'll!" Clare's shrill voice is frantic in Lola's head.

What the...?

Lola's tires squeal.

Boom! The Jeep hits a granite post in the college entryway.

It's finally silent.

Acknowledgements

I'd like to thank all those who made this book possible and such joy to write, particularly those in an online identity disorder support group whose courageous stories continue to inspire Lola's journey. For me, Host is about something we all have in common – a shared need to discover and understand who we truly are. Stay true to yourselves and honor your unique voices.

In no specific order, my love and gratitude go out to the following:

Special thanks to my editor, Toni Rakestraw, who has taught me everything you'd ever want to know about point of view. Thank you to the team at Limitless, who work so hard to help make writers' dreams come true.

For my other Maria – You took me under your wing and used humor to help me through self-doubt.
For my other Tim – Who never let me lose sight of my dreams and never will.

*For my other Clare – You remind me
of my youth and dare me to dream in
color.*
*For my other Zoe – Your ability to
understand me makes me wonder if you
were my own alter in another life.*
*For my other Frog – I remind myself
of how you always keep hopping, even
when you want to give up. I admire you.*
*For my other Rabbit – Your bravery
humbles me. Someday, I'll write a book
just for you.*
*For my other Samantha – I miss you. I
write to bring your spirit back.*

About the Author

Erin Lee is a freelance writer and therapist living with her family in Southern New Hampshire. She is the author of *Crazy Like Me*, a novel published in 2015 by Savant Books and Publications, LLC and *Wave to Papa*, 2015 and *Nine Lives*, 2016 by Limitless Publishing. She has also published numerous magazine articles, particularly on the topic of mental illness. She holds a master's degree in psychology and works with at-risk families and as a court appointed special children's advocate.

Preview of *Host*, book two in the "Lola Party of Eight" series by Erin Lee:

Chapter One:
Waking Up Lola

The sterile smell of hospital floor cleaner and the tooting of monitoring machinery wakes Lola with a start. She opens her eyes slowly, knowing something is off. She lies in bed with a green-checkered curtain around her. Loud coughing from the other side of the curtain tell her she isn't in her bed at her mother's house. The monitors grow even louder as her eyes open. With each beep, she feels something digging deeper into her head. She groans in agony. Her mind flashes back to the time she got a concussion playing field hockey in junior high school. That's how this feels. The threat of bile in her stomach coming up confirms she's in a similar state now. She forces the bile down and takes a deep breath. She knows she's in a hospital, but why? She misses Maria and wishes the alters hadn't merged.

She quickly scans her mental rolodex for what could have happened. The last thing she remembers is driving home from the pharmacy. *Or was it school? Was I registering for school?*

Lola immediately sits up. She checks both ankles and both wrists and is relieved to see they aren't strapped to the bed. *What happened? Where am I? Why am I here? Am I still at Rosewood?*

"Oh, Honey! You're *awake! Wonderful!*" her mother—Stella's—panicked voice turns soft as she hustles past machines and chairs in the cramped space to take a closer look at her daughter's face.

"Mom...why am I here?" Lola asks abruptly, not giving her mother space to say anything more until her questions are answered.

"You had a car accident," Stella says. "You're okay. No big deal. We can replace your car. I'm just *so* glad you're okay!"

"A car accident? When? Why? Was anyone hurt?" the questions tumble from Lola's mouth faster than she can think them through. The last time she was in a car accident, she was 16, and lost her best friend, Holly. It was an accident that changed her life—so many lives—forever.

"You know, Lola, I thought that when you were all grown up it wouldn't be your job anymore to give me all my gray hairs."

Stella laughs, running her fingers through her long salty hair. Despite it all, at over seventy years old, Stella doesn't look a day over fifty-five. "Charlotte's in the waiting room right now, do you want me to get her?"

Answer me! Lola wants to scream. *It has to be pretty bad if she's calling Charlotte and bothering her. Charlotte has shit to do. Charlotte has a life.* Lola wants answers. *Now*. But her head hurts. She wiggles her toes; just to be sure they work. *Thank God.*

"Please just stay with me for now, Mom. I'm feeling a little fuzzy," Lola says; feeling like a ten-year-old, hoping this feeling won't cause a new alter to emerge—something that's happened many times before.

"Okay, Dragonfly," Stella says.

Let's try this again. "What exactly happened?" Lola asks, rubbing her forehead and laying back into her bed. The sudden movement weakens her and her stomach lurches. Lola grimaces.

"You were driving to the college and must have blacked out or something. Maybe it was your meds? They found Xanax in your purse. Other prescriptions too. We aren't sure. You ran into the big sign in the entrance. That archway thing,"

Stella says. "No one else was hurt but you hit your head pretty hard on the steering wheel. How are you feeling?"

Things began to click. Lola had signed up for some classes at the community college. It was all part of her plan, something her therapist had suggested after finally reclaiming her life after thirty years in a mental hospital. *Jesus, talk about making an entrance! Classes for second fall semester term haven't even started yet.*

"How much damage?" Lola asks, not sure she is ready for the answer.

"Well, the sign's pretty banged up and I think the Jeep will be totaled. But those things don't matter. The damage to *you* was pretty minimal. The doctors think it's just a bad concussion. You'll be able to go home today if the doctor releases you," Stella says. "I don't think I could stand you being hospitalized for one more night. Been there, done that—for, oh, three decades. All set."

Lola's confused. She scratches her head, but rethinks it when pain comes rushing toward her temples. *Just a concussion? Why do I feel so out of it? Why can't I remember driving to the college or the accident?*

Stella is saying "just a concussion," but Lola can tell by the circles under her mother's eyes that she hasn't slept. Lola's natural empathy—often dreaded—kicks in. She smiles at her mother, ignoring her own throbbing head and worries. She reaches for Stella's hand.

"Don't worry, Mom. I'm okay. *Stop looking so worried.* When will the doctor be back?" Lola asks, not sure she believes a word of the reassurances she gifts her mother. Stella smiles at her only biological child and exhales.

"You can go get Charlotte now if you want," Lola says finally.

"I'll be right back! She's really worried. She'll be so happy to see you," Stella says, opening the privacy curtain and slipping out like a Las Vegas magician.

I must look horrible. "Okay, Mom," Lola says to her mother's retreating frame. She takes a deep breath to calm her anxieties and attempts to find the reason for her crash. She knows she's a safe driver and she's confident she hadn't taken Xanax before getting behind the wheel. She only took that on an as needed basis and never more than one pill at a time. *Why can't I remember?*

Stella isn't gone more than five minutes before returning with Lola's step-sister Charlotte. Charlotte is dressed in a black and gray pencil skirt with a white blouse and a women's suit jacket that matches her skirt perfectly. How she manages to look professional and be comfortable all at once is a miracle to Lola. *Clare would die if she saw that outfit*, Lola thinks. *She's been trying to get me to want to dress like that for years. As if it matters how you look in a nuthouse...*

"Are you trying to kill us all?" Charlotte laughs, her voice anything but professional, fully entering Lola's emergency room makeshift cubicle.

Lola laughs.

"Yes! That's it. That's what this is all about," Lola says, rubbing her forehead again. "Holy hell this is sore. How long have I been here?"

"Since yesterday. Pathetic, right? They still haven't even gotten you a room. Mom is fit to be tied! Any minute, she's going to break out the voodoo dolls and cast a spell on these nurses." Charlotte warns.

Lola wants to laugh but can't. The concept of having her own room in another hospital isn't something she can laugh about. Charlotte, who's only ever been in the hospital for an overnight here or there or to have her children, doesn't understand how terrifying this is for Lola. "I have to get out of here, Char," she confesses. "I'm totally freaked out. I don't remember the accident, really. I mean, kind of. But not like I probably should. How do you know they won't keep me here?"

"Don't worry about that. They said a day or two. They just need to make sure your concussion is all set. Your CAT scan came back normal, so I'm thinking you'll be out of here sooner rather than later. If you want, I can let the nurses know that you're awake and alert again. Maybe they can get the doctor in here to talk to you? You keep sorta drifting off and they thought maybe it was just…well, you know…your other thing," Charlotte says.

Lola winces, knowing her step-sister is doing her best to be nice and not mention the elephant in the room—her Dissociative Identity Disorder (DID) diagnosis. Only four months ago, Lola had been a long-term patient at Rosewood Hospital for Mental Wellness doing everything in her power to get her seven alter egos to merge so she could finally be released and begin a life of her own. With her alters merged into one personality—hers—she's spent the last four months trying to piece her life back together; not an easy task. Hearing

Charlotte bring up the diagnosis gives her a flashback she wishes was only a bad dream:

Lola thinks about Edna—a fellow Rosewood patient—as she drives her new Jeep to the community college to register for a class. We're all the same. And we're all going to be okay.

"But not me! I'm not going to be okay! It's boring as hell in here, ya'll!" Clare's shrill voice is frantic in Lola's head.

What the…?

Lola's tires squeal.

Boom! The Jeep hits a granite post in the college entryway.

It's finally silent.

Lola tries to tell herself it can't be true. That it can't have been hearing Clare's voice after four months of silence that caused her accident. She looks at Charlotte, nodding, and pretending to understand what she's saying. But inside, Lola knows the truth. Her alters are back—Clare anyway—and they won't be going anywhere anytime soon.

***

My name is Lola Murray. I'm 52 years old and suffer from DID and about ten other mental issues. I don't really care about the labels. The whole thing is both ridiculous and embarrassing at this point. What I care about is what it's like living with seven other people, called alters or alter egos, in my brain. I thought I had them gone. I thought we'd made a deal—they'd merge and we'd become one personality and finally do something with our lives—but I was wrong, clearly. Tonight, I'm in the hospital after a car accident. Apparently, I ran into a brick entrance at the local college because my wildest alter—Clare—decided she couldn't stay quiet any longer. I can't say I haven't missed her, but she just set us all back by four months at least. Now, I don't know what to do with myself or them. She hasn't spoken since. Maybe it was just a one-time thing.

My family just left and are excited about me getting out of here tomorrow. I don't know if I should be going anywhere, not with my alters back. My family doesn't know my alters well. They called them my "invisible friends" when I was a kid. They won't know how to deal with them—with me—if the alters are here to stay. I'm terrified. If I tell anyone about them, they will likely send me right back to the mental hospital. If I don't, I'll have to keep this secret—not an easy task when you have people living inside you who won't stay quiet and personalities all their own.

I'm trying to convince myself that I didn't really hear Clare's voice. That I just imagined it. Or maybe it was the meds. Maybe I just missed her so much that I wanted to hear her. It would be so much easier if any of these stories I'm telling myself are true. But the thing with this disease is that you don't mistake your alters' voices. They are real in every way. I can't tell you how many years I spent trying to convince the doctors at Rosewood of this. It's no different for me to talk to my alters than it is for normal people to talk to their friends or family. Only these friends and family live in my head and I'm the only one who can hear them. Worse, they sometimes take over and speak for me. If anything, that makes them more real, not less.

I just spent four months and days on end in therapy doing everything I could to start my life over. Do you have any idea what that's like at my age? I don't even know who I am. For nearly forty years, I've had other people inside of me telling me who I am. Anything and everything I did was by committee decision. It's only in these last few months that I've been able to make choices of my own. And I'm pretty proud of what I've done. I finally got my driver's license, something I started working on at age sixteen, right before the accident that killed Holly. I also got registered for classes and a part time job. I was beginning to make plans to move out of my mother's house. After all, she's in her seventies. I can't be living with her forever. This is humiliating enough.

The last four months have been the bravest and most empowering of my life. And now it's all at risk. If Clare really did talk to me, freak me out, and cause that accident, it means the others will follow behind her soon. I'm surprised I haven't heard from Maria. She's the oldest of my alters and is always around when I'm hurting. I keep telling myself that if the alters were really back, Maria would be here now, asking me how my head felt. So maybe it's okay. Maybe I just imagined Clare and there's nothing to worry about. Maria wouldn't just leave me here. She's too much of a worrier.

Do you have any idea how much work it took to get the alters to merge? I should have known it couldn't—wouldn't—last. The classic therapeutic metaphor for a patient with DID is of a broken vase.

People think you can break a vase and just pick it up and glue all its pieces back together, right? So, in human terms, with DID patients, the alters are the broken pieces. They think that you can identify all the shards and fragments of the original personality and, using the glue of talk therapy, hypnosis, drugs, and determination, throw them all together back into a pretty vase. Yeah, right. Doesn't work like that. The vase probably still leaks. And that's where I'm likely at now—Clare being the first of many drips and drops to come.

Even if you aren't bothered by drips and drops, you can smash a vase, bury it in the ground, dig it up later, and put it together again. You can do that because the pieces don't change in size and shape. With personality pieces, you have a problem because they are alive and they change and grow with life experiences. The pieces never fit back together just right. I feel like an absolute fool for not realizing it would only be a matter of time before I was soaking wet.

Now, I have to figure out what to do. Being here, listening to the beeps and buzzing, the hallway lights and a roommate who won't stop snoring, is only making me feel crazier than I already know I am. I keep telling myself it's only one night and that I'll be home by tomorrow. I tell myself I'm not even on the psych ward and they're only monitoring me to be sure I don't run into problems with bleeding or something. I feel like an idiot for disassociating. Had I not done that, I'd be home at Mom's with a bag of peas on my head. But when you have as many mental issues as I do, it's not as easy as it sounds to stay cool.

There's no chance I'll sleep tonight. I wouldn't have slept at Mom's, either. I have too much to decide. I could tell my group what's happening. They would understand. Many of them have alters—or did—and would totally get it. They'd say this is normal and my fears are normal. But they aren't the ones who just did thirty *years* in a nuthouse. Most of them got out in under a year. They don't understand just *how* crazy I am. I could tell my therapist— any one of them—but they would report it and that would land me right back in my old room at Rosewood. I wonder if Tina's still there. Maybe we could be roommates again. Or worse, they'd put me with old lady Edna; asking me if we're going to die every thirty seconds. Asking me if we are okay. This time, I'll scream, "No, Edna! We are clearly *not* okay!"

251

If I don't tell, it could go even worse, though, because I'll be alone with them; trying to cover for them. They will come, one by one, and begin to stake their claim in my life. Maria will want to take over, saying she's protecting me and making me take things slow. I don't have time to take anything slow. I haven't even had a chance to live. Zoe and Clare, on the other hand, will want me to make up for lost time and have me out in bars and at auditions before Monday morning. Frog and Tim will want me researching sex changes and Rabbit will likely try to kill us all by Friday. I do miss Sam. It might be nice to see her. To see how she likes living on the outside. Maybe, if I could just reason with them, we could work something out? I've got to get out of here. For today and tomorrow, at least, I'm going to have to keep my mouth shut and wait until I—we—have some time to think of something, anything. I'm just not sure I can handle this alone.

ERIN LEE's work can be found at:
www.authorerinlee.com,
on Goodreads, Author Erin Lee,
on Facebook at:
www.facebook.com/gonecrazytalksoon
and on twitter at @Crazylikeme2015.

***

This is a work of fiction. Names, characters, places, and incidents are either

the product of the author's imagination or
are used fictitiously and/or have been
altered to suit the story.

***